Those Who Are IGNORANT

DAG HEWARD-MILLS

Parchment House

Unless otherwise stated, all Scripture quotations are taken from the
King James Version of the Bible

Excerpts in Chapter 1 taken from The Final Quest by Rick Joyner.
(Excerpts taken from Part 1 - "The Hordes of Hell are Marching", Pages
16-19) Originally published: 2nd Ed. © 1996. Used by permission of
Morning Star Publications & Ministries, P.O. Box 19409, Charlotte, NC
28219-9409, Order Department: 1-800-542-0278; Fax: 1-704-522-7212

First published 2008 by Lux Verbi.BM (Pty) Ltd.
PO Box 5, Wellington 7654, South Africa
Reg no 1953/000037/07
2nd Printing 2008

This edition published by Parchment House
3rd Printing 2014
ISBN : 978-9988-8569-7-7

Find out more about Dag Heward-Mills at:
Healing Jesus Campaign

Write to: evangelist@daghewardmills.org
Website: www.daghewardmills.org
Facebook: Dag Heward-Mills
Twitter: @EvangelistDag

Dedication : *To Rev. Robert Dodoo*
Thank you for being my brother and my best man.

Contents

1. Ignorance and Disloyalty 1

2. Ten Laws of Loyalty 9

3. Five Rules of Loyalty 41

4. Six Principles of Loyalty 51

5. Three Causes of Disloyalty 70

6. The Timing of Disloyalty 81

7. Six Manifestations of Disloyalty 88

8. The Loyalty of Christ 93

9. The Loyalty of the Father 105

10. The Three Tests of Loyalty 114

11. The Rewards of Loyalty 121

12. Seven Methods for Dealing with Disloyalty 125

Chapter 1

Ignorance and Disloyalty

But if any man be ignorant, let him be ignorant.
1 Corinthians 14:38

There is much to be learned about loyalty and disloyalty. There are many ignorant people who choose to be ignorant still even though there is a lot to be learned. This book contains the principles, laws, rules and facts that govern the concepts of loyalty and disloyalty. Disloyalty is often a fruit of ignorance, immaturity and even a lack of education. Uneducated people are more prone to rebellion and disloyalty because they do not understand the implications of what they are doing. Through the teachings of this book, you will overcome the disadvantages that ignorance brings to your life and ministry.

More churches are destroyed by the work of disloyalty than by anything else I know! I found that out first hand in the first year of my ministry. My fledgling ministry experienced a satanic attack through conspiracy, accusations, faultfinding, slander and breakaways. I have never seen as much confusion as I saw in those days.

Very early in the ministry, I came to the conclusion that disloyalty and its associated evils are the most destructive weapons in the devil's armoury.

Most Christians feel that the devil's best weapon is to work through occultism, witchcraft and voodoo. I agree that these things are weapons in the devil's arsenal.

But what people must realize is that the strongest campaign of Satan is in the area of deception. If Satan can deceive you, he will destroy you! Satan makes many people believe that they are fighting a man of God in the name of justice and truth. However, they soon discover with great pain, that they are doing nothing but kicking their feet against nails and thorns.

This is what Paul discovered when he fought against the church and supervised the elimination of one of its leaders, Stephen. Saul was a man with a good conscience. He earnestly thought that he was eliminating troublemakers from the peaceful city of Jerusalem. In his fight for righteousness, he sought to wipe out elements that he thought were harmful to society. There are many people who think they are on a holy war to expose false preachers and ministries. **Like Saul, they think they have a divine mandate to let everyone know the truth about the hypocrites in the pulpits.** The Apostle Paul was so surprised to find out that he was actually fighting against Christ.

> **And as he journeyed, he came near Damascus: and suddenly there shined round about him a light from heaven: And he fell to the earth, and heard a voice saying unto him, Saul, Saul, why persecutest thou me? And he said, Who art thou, Lord? And the Lord said, I am Jesus whom thou persecutest: it is hard for thee to kick against the pricks. And he TREMBLING AND ASTONISHED said, Lord, what will thou have me to do...**
>
> Acts 9:3-6

Paul was astonished when he discovered what he was really doing! When people do not know what they are doing, they often do the wrong thing. Paul claimed later on that he had received mercy from God because he did not know what he was doing.

> **Who was before a blasphemer, and a persecuter, and injurious: but I obtained mercy, because I DID IT IGNORANTLY IN UNBELIEF.**
>
> 1 Timothy 1:13

The inability to be faithful, loyal, stable, consistent and constant is the greatest killer of ministries. It is the greatest killer of businesses. The feeling that there is a shorter, quicker and easier way is in all men. Satan capitalizes on that tendency.

Many Christians are tricked into following rebels and dissident visionaries. Many people do these things out of ignorance. The devil uses the example of tyrannical church leaders to create the culture of rebellion and disloyalty in the church. Without knowing it, many church leaders are essentially rebellious and disloyal. They teach their followers rebellion by the things they say and do. They do not understand why anyone is unfaithful or disloyal to them. You see, deception is such a strong thing. When you are deceived you think that black is white and white is black.

A Vision of Disloyalty

I was really intrigued by the revelation that the Lord gave to Rick Joyner in his book "The Final Quest". He described a vision of a large demonic army marching against the church. The main aim of this demonic army was to cause division on every possible level of relationship: churches with other churches, congregations with their pastors and even husbands with their wives.

Another notable aspect of the revelation was the weapons that this demonic army was carrying. I noted in particular that the spears they were carrying were called 'treachery'. Do you know that treachery is actually the highest form of disloyalty? It is interesting to me that only one spear was named and that spear was treachery! Dear friend, I believe that Satan's principal spear against the church is this weapon of disloyalty and treachery.

As I mused over this, I realized that many churches that had suffered major setbacks, had suffered these things because of disloyalty and treachery. I thought about several great men of God I had grown to respect and considered how their ministries had become stunted. Disloyalty had played a major role in this regrettable turn of events.

There were four arrows mentioned in the vision: *accusation, gossip, slander* and *faultfinding*. On the surface, these four weapons do not sound very effective. *They do not even sound like weapons the devil would use.* However, after being in the ministry for some years I have concluded that the most potent weapons of the devil are these very things. At first glance, most inexperienced people would dismiss these as minor problems.

I am sure that many people have considered these listed arrows as trivial things that every minister can easily handle. The devil knows that accusations weaken, confuse and paralyse the accused person. No matter how innocent the accused person is, once he is accused he is drawn into a state of confusion. He asks himself, "Why would anybody think of such a thing?" Accusations are so powerful that, after a while, even innocent people begin to agree with the accusations. Accusations paralyse the accused person. Once paralysed, they are left in a state of inactivity. As the accusations spread, the accused person does not even have the confidence to move in the circles where the venom has been spread. Slander, gossip and faultfinding are all forms of accusation. These things weaken, paralyse and confuse the church. This confusion is within and without the church. The accused person is confused and the hearers are confused. Many people never overcome this confusion. Some can never receive and some cannot continue in ministry. This is such a powerful weapon of the enemy! It is no wonder the Bible tells us that strength comes to the church when the accuser is dealt with. As long as you hear the voice of the accuser, you will be weakened somewhat.

> **And I heard a loud voice saying in heaven, Now is come salvation, and STRENGTH... for the accuser of our brethren is cast down, which accused them before our God day and night.**
>
> **Revelation 12:10**

Have you ever wondered why relentless accusations are hurled at men of God? I remember a pastor who did a great pioneering work in a large city. Through him, many people were saved and many other ministers were trained. He was slandered and accused until he eventually left the city. His faults were magnified until there was nothing good said about him anymore. Eventually, he left the city and put aside the ministry. Satan's modus operandi is quite simple – accuse them until they have no confidence in themselves! Accuse them until no one in the community thinks well of them. Make them stop what they are doing.

However, many years after leaving, he was invited back and honoured by the people he had blessed. I believe he was surprised when he saw the fruit of his ministry. He probably realized that he should not have succumbed to the relentless onslaught of the accuser and his agents. I am glad to say that soon after this he returned to the ministry.

Another amazing revelation in this book was that the demons were riding on Christians and not on horses. In other words, Christians were being used by the devil without even knowing it!

I know a pastor who is very good at dividing the Body of Christ. I have observed his ministry over the last fifteen years and I feel he has a special gift for dividing the church and creating opposing "camps" within the church. I think he does not even know that his actions and decisions lead to the creation of factions within the church. He does this effortlessly and with such distinguished diplomacy! He looks and sounds so respectable that it would never occur to you that he is actually splitting the church into groups. It is only when you sit back and reflect on his actions that you realize how factious he is.

I include here a short passage from Rick Joyner's vision of the armies of Satan. I pray that you will see the strategies of the devil clearly.

> *"The demonic army was so large that it stretched as far as I could see. It was separated into divisions, with each carrying a different banner. The foremost divisions marched under the banners of Pride, Self-righteousness, Respectability, Selfish Ambition, Unrighteous Judgment, and Jealousy. There were many more of these evil divisions beyond my scope of vision, but those in the vanguard of this terrible horde from hell seemed to be the most powerful. The leader of this army was the Accuser of the Brethren himself.*
>
> *The weapons carried by this horde were also named. The swords were named Intimidation; the spears were named Treachery; and the arrows were named Accusation, Gossip, Slander and Faultfinding. Scouts and smaller companies of demons with such names as Rejection, Bitterness, Impatience,*

Unforgiveness and Lust were sent in advance of this army to prepare for the main attack.

These smaller companies and scouts were much fewer in number, but they were no less powerful than some of the larger divisions that followed. They were smaller only for strategic reasons. Just as John the Baptist was a single man, but was given an extraordinary anointing for baptizing the masses to prepare them for the Lord, these smaller demonic companies were given extraordinary evil powers for "baptizing the masses." A single demon of Bitterness could sow his poison into multitudes of people, even entire races or cultures. A demon of Lust would attach himself to a single performer, movie, or even advertisement, and send what appeared to be bolts of electric slime that would hit and "desensitise" great masses of people. All of this was to prepare for the great horde of evil which followed.

This army was marching specifically against the church, but it was attacking everyone that it could. I knew that it was seeking to pre-empt a coming move of God which was destined to sweep masses of people into the church.

The primary strategy of this army was to cause division on every possible level of relationship – churches with each other, congregations with their pastors, husbands and wives, children and parents, and even children with each other. The scouts were sent to locate the openings in churches, families or individuals that Rejection, Bitterness, Lust, etc., could exploit and make larger. Then the following divisions would pour through the openings to completely overcome their victims.

The most shocking part of this vision was that this horde was not riding on horses, but primarily on Christians! Most of them were well-dressed, respectable, and had the appearance of being refined and educated, but there also seemed to be representatives from almost every walk of life. These people professed Christian truths in order to appease their consciences, but they lived their lives in agreement with the powers of darkness. As they agreed with those powers their assigned demons grew and more easily directed their actions.

Many of these believers were host to more than one demon, but one would obviously be in charge. The nature of the one in charge dictated which division it was marching in. Even though the divisions were all marching together, it also seemed that at the same time the entire army was on the verge of chaos. For example, the demons of hate, hated the other demons as much as they did the Christians. The demons of jealousy were all jealous of one another.

The only way the leaders of this horde kept the demons from fighting each other was to keep their hatred, jealousy, etc., focused on the people they were riding. However, these people would often break out in fights with each other. I knew that this was how some of the armies that had come against Israel in the Scriptures had ended up destroying themselves. When their purpose against Israel was thwarted, their rage was uncontrollable, and they simply began fighting each other.

I noted that the demons were riding on these Christians, but were not in them as was the case with non-Christians. It was obvious that these believers had only to stop agreeing with their demons in order to get free of them. For example, if the Christian on which a demon of jealousy was riding just started to question the jealousy, that demon would weaken very fast. When this happened the weakening demon would cry out and the leader of the division would direct all of the demons around that Christian to attack him until the bitterness, etc., would build up on him again. If this did not work, the demons would begin quoting Scriptures that were perverted in such a way that would justify the bitterness, accusations, etc.

It was clear that the power of the demons was rooted almost entirely in the power of deception, but they had deceived these Christians to the point where they could use them and they would think they were being used by God. This was because banners of Self-righteousness were being carried by almost all of the individuals so that those marching could not even see the banners that marked the true nature of these divisions.

As I looked far to the rear of this army I saw the entourage of the Accuser himself. I began to understand his strategy, and I was amazed that it was so simple. He knew that a house divided cannot stand, and this army represented an

7

attempt to bring such division to the church that she would completely fall from grace. It was apparent that the only way he could do this was to use Christians to war against their own brethren, and that is why almost everyone in the forward divisions were Christians, or at least professing Christians. Every step that these deceived believers took in obedience to the Accuser strengthened his power over them. This made his confidence and the confidence of all of his commanders grow with the progress of the army as it marched forward. It was apparent that the power of this army depended on the agreement of these Christians with the ways of evil."

Chapter 2

Ten Laws of Loyalty

1. The Head of an Organisation Must First Be Loyal to His Subordinates

L oyalty does not just depend on the subordinates being loyal to their superior. Everything, good or bad, flows down from the top.

It is like the precious ointment UPON THE HEAD, THAT RAN DOWN upon the beard...THAT WENT DOWN to the skirts...

Psalm 133:2

Whatever is at the top, will be found in the ranks. The starting point of loyalty is the head of the organisation. If he is unfaithful to his followers, they will be unfaithful to him.

Can I Be Loyal to this Man?

This is why it is difficult to teach loyalty in some churches. Some churches have unreasonable pastors. Some churches have leaders who are disloyal to their subordinates in many ways. **It is difficult or impossible to teach people to be loyal to a disloyal head.** The overseer may be someone who is not kind to his associates and does not even speak well of them.

I was once chatting with a senior pastor. He spoke about my associates.

He said, "You have all these nice people working with you. They are so loyal." Then he lamented; "But I have all these devils as associates, I wish I had people like yours."

I thought to myself; "If you call your associates devils, what do you expect from them?" Perhaps it had not occurred to him that if his pastors were devils then he must be Lucifer! Just as

9

a loyal subordinate should not speak evil of his senior, the head must also not speak evil of his subordinates. Not only was it inappropriate for him to speak like that about his subordinates, but also, it was not appropriate for him to say such things to an outsider.

I heard another overseer refer to his branch pastors as "wicked people" and as "wizards". Just as the junior pastors should not refer to their senior as a wizard or a wicked man, this should also not come from the top.

Why People Leave Organisations!

It is very difficult to live under certain kinds of leadership. There is a reason why Africans flood western nations seeking greener pastures. They are not running away from their homes and families. They are not running away from the weather in Africa. They are not running away from their friends. They are running away from bad leaders!

It is difficult to live under leadership which is oppressive. It is difficult to live under leaders who steal the nation's wealth and do not care if the people have roads, hospitals and schools for their children. It is difficult to live in an environment where you do not have great opportunities. I know that most Ghanaians would come back to their own country if they could.

The Greatest Motivation for Employees!

It has been noted that the greatest motivation for people in work places, is not money per se. A sense of self-worth and achievement is the highest motivation for workers.

If someone does not feel important and appreciated, he often begins to look elsewhere. **It is the duty of the head of the organisation (church or business) to make everyone feel important and appreciated. This is one of the most important ways to be loyal to the people who work under you.**

When I worked as a doctor for Ghana's Ministry of Health, I felt that the government did not care about me. After slaving away for one year, I decided that it would be better for me to sell groundnuts at the roadside, than to work for the Ministry of Health. I was not loyal to the Ministry of Health. It took me only one year to leave them. I moved away quietly and I have no regrets.

The head of the organisation often wants his subordinates to appreciate him and honour him. **However, this appreciation and honour must begin from the head downwards.** I reiterate that it is difficult and sometimes impossible, to work under certain kinds of leadership. If you are a junior in a church or business and have a head who is uncaring, you will have a hard time. I would advise you to find the environment and leader under whom you can flourish. Move away peacefully and do not say bad things on your way out! Close every door gently! You may need to come back through that door one day.

Why I Am Loyal to You!

One day a young pastor asked his senior pastor, "Do you know why I am loyal to you?" The senior pastor smiled and asked, "Why?" The junior pastor said, "I think the main reason why I am loyal to you is because you are a very loyal senior minister." He continued, "It is not because I have learnt the lessons or stages of loyalty. But because you are very loyal to me." He added, "I feel that you have my welfare at heart. I feel that you want me to prosper. I sense that you want me to go as far as I possibly can. Because of this, I naturally find myself being loyal to you." This young pastor was unknowingly expounding on a great principle of loyalty.

Loyalty emanates from the head. Loyalty breeds more loyalty!

Consider this: is it easy to follow someone who constantly turns round and waves a knife at you? Would you be able to stay close to someone who constantly waves a dangerous dagger in your direction? Certainly not! In the same way, it is not easy to be loyal to wicked leaders (even if they are men of God).

11

I have often said that if I were not a pastor, I would find it difficult to remain in certain churches. I would find it very difficult to be loyal to pastors I did not believe in.

Moreover it is required in stewards, that a man be found faithful.

1 Corinthians
4:2

One of the cardinal qualifications for the head of every organisation is loyalty!

2. Loyalty Is the Key to Expansion

Many churches, businesses and individuals need to tap into the key of loyalty in order to expand. Growth in one location can take place only up to a point. That is what we call localized growth. You sell a product but only a certain number of people can buy the product in one locality. After a while the community will be saturated with what you are selling. That is why you need to expand. Often, expansion takes place in different geographical locations.

Years ago, our church was directed by the Lord to expand into different communities in the city. This has resulted in tremendous growth. Had we stayed in one place, we would have had one congregation probably of the same size that we have now.

But I followed the direction of the Holy Spirit and moved into several localities within the city. Today the strength of Lighthouse Chapel International has immensely multiplied into the different communities of our city. Not only have we expanded in the city, we have also expanded into several regions of our nation Ghana and into several other countries. Lighthouse Chapel International now operates on five continents: Africa, Europe, America, Asia and Australia. We are in more than twenty different countries of the world. These are not local churches that have adopted the Lighthouse name. They are extensions, outreaches and expansions of the original Lighthouse Chapel International, which began in Korle-Bu, Accra, Ghana.

People often ask, "How are you able to maintain your operations in all these different places?" The key is loyalty.

If you are a businessman, and have a shop in an area, you can only make a certain amount of money from one community. You need to expand into other localities. God is a God of expansion. God wants you to have big dreams. That is why He told Adam and Eve to fill the whole Earth. How could two people fill the whole Earth with human beings? But that was God's plan for Adam and Eve.

You can fill the city with your shops, businesses or whatever you trade in. If you are a pastor, what you are doing can be expanded into many places. You can have many churches. As I write this book, there are over four hundred Lighthouse churches in the world. It is possible to expand but you must grasp the principles that make expansion possible. One of the keys to expansion and growth is loyalty.

You will need loyal people at all the outlets you establish. Without loyal people in position, everything you do will crumble after a while. I know churches which do not even want to have cell groups. They have had bad experiences with disloyal people who have turned their cell groups into rebellious offshoots. Many church planters have watched as satellite or branch churches have been taken over by anarchistic pastors. These pastors have no respect for authority or order in the church.

I know a pastor who began a church twice in a city but had to close them down because the church was overrun by 'rebels'. This general overseer is no longer interested in church planting or church expansion. He is content to stay with what he can control in one locality. In this book, I want to share with you the Lord's principles and tenets of loyalty. If I were a businessman, I would prefer to have one loyal person without a degree than three with MBA's and PhD's. Qualifications do not impress me as much as loyalty does.

Many years ago, my father owned a prestigious hotel in the city of Accra. My father would supervise this hotel by visiting it once or twice a day. Unknown to him the managers and workers in the hotel were ripping him off. Whilst he was away, customers would check into the hotel. However, the money they paid never got to my father because the staff at the hotel did not register the guests in the proper way. One day something happened and my father dismissed all the management staff. My father asked me if I knew somebody who could manage the hotel. I said to him, "Well, I know someone who would be honest and loyal to you. But he doesn't have any experience in managing a hotel."My father answered, "Please bring him. I need him now!"

So I called my friend and he agreed to do the job for a while. After this friend of mine had worked for one night, the hotel yielded about one hundred and fifty thousand cedis. Previously it had yielded only ten thousand cedis a night.

There was a sudden 150% increase in the income of the hotel!! Can you imagine that! These qualified managers had adroitly stolen large amounts of money.

The introduction of one loyal person made an amazing difference to the income of that business. Dear business friend, dear politician, the introduction of loyal people into your field of work will tremendously affect your output and your profit.

Many people do not value honesty and loyalty. But we would do well to learn from Jesus. Jesus did not go for qualifications. He went for loyalty and faithfulness. Look at what Paul said about employees or stewards.

Moreover, it is required in stewards, that a man be found faithful.

1 Corinthians 4:2

Loyalty is necessary for your expansion. It is required for your business. It is required for your church. With all your getting, get loyalty. Understand the principles that govern loyalty. Discover the laws of loyalty and disloyalty. God will bless the work of your hands and expand it greatly.

3. Loyalty Breeds Loyalty

You must be loyal to several people. You must be loyal to your God, you must be loyal to your church, you must be loyal to your spouse and you must be loyal to your friends.

A leader breeds loyalty by being loyal to the people who follow him. When it is time for your followers to be rewarded, be faithful and let the rewards materialize. Do not withhold the blessings of those who have laboured with you for years. When one of your followers is in trouble, that is the time to show your loyalty. Dear friend, your followers are watching you closely. They will do what they see. If you do not betray them in their time of difficulty, they will not betray you. Loyalty breeds loyalty!

A leader breeds loyalty in his followers by being loyal to his superiors. When David had the opportunity to kill Saul, he did not! He was loyal to the king's authority. He did not execute his own father. And all his men saw it.

Then said Abishai to David, God hath delivered thine enemy into thine hand this day; now therefore let me smite him, I pray thee, with the spear even to the earth at once, and I will not smite him the second time. And David said to Abishai, Destroy him not: for who can stretch forth his hand against the Lord's anointed, and be guiltless? David said furthermore, As the Lord liveth, the Lord shall smite him; or his day shall come to die; or he shall descend into battle, and perish. THE LORD FORBID THAT I SHOULD STRETCH FORTH MINE HAND AGAINST THE LORD'S ANOINTED: but, I pray thee, take thou now the spear that is at his bolster, and the cruse of water, and let us go.

1 Samuel 26:8-11

Many years later, David himself made a mistake. He murdered one of his own soldiers called Uriah. David could have lost his life through that mistake. Many of his leaders could have revolted and assassinated him. However, this did not happen. His men were loyal to the king's authority. They refused to kill the Lord's anointed because they had learnt it by example many years earlier. They had learnt not to 'kill' fathers.

A leader breeds loyalty by being loyal to his friends. When David became the king, he realized that his position was truly a privileged one. In the midst of his establishment as a leader, he asked for a way he could show kindness to an old friend.

And David said, Is there yet any that is left of the house of Saul, that I may show him kindness for Jonathan's sake?

2 Samuel 9:1

These acts of loyalty to friends teach others about the true character of the leader they are dealing with. People are attracted to a good character. People are more inclined to follow someone with a good heart.

A leader breeds loyalty by being loyal to his spouse. Because marriage is such a difficult thing for many people, anyone who has his marriage in order is seen as a natural leader. You become a natural leader in the community because it is evident that your domestic affairs are under control. Loyalty to your spouse involves self-control and discipline. Everyone would like to have a leader with these qualities.

A bishop then must be blameless, the HUSBAND OF ONE WIFE, vigilant, sober, of good behaviour, given to hospitality, apt to teach; One that RULETH WELL HIS OWN HOUSE, having his children in subjection with all gravity; (For if a man know not how to rule his own house, how shall he take care of the church of God?)

1 Timothy 3:2, 4, 5

A leader breeds loyalty by being loyal to his own vision. Nobody wants to follow someone who is unpredictable. Many years ago, I declared my interest in soul winning and establishing people in Christ. I am still doing the same thing. Much water has passed under the bridge but the vision is still the same – a soul is a soul and is precious to God. He may be a beggar, a lawyer or a doctor – a soul is a soul and is precious to God. She may be a groundnut seller, a prostitute or a nurse – a soul is a soul and is precious to God.

Keep the same vision. The Bible teaches that you should not associate with people who are prone to sudden mutations and unexpected twists and turns. It is dangerous to sit in a car with a driver who makes dangerous sharp turns.

My son, fear thou the Lord and the king: and meddle not with them that are given to change:

Proverbs 24:21

Are you a leader? Develop a group of faithful, stable, constant and loyal followers by being a loyal person yourself.

Finally, a leader breeds loyalty by being loyal to God. When you study the Bible, you will discover that rebellions were often instigated against people who were not following the will of God. Let me clarify an important point here. I am not saying that anyone who experiences betrayals, rebellions and disloyalty is out of the will of God. If that was the case, then Almighty God was doing something wrong when Lucifer rebelled. If that was the case, than Jesus was doing something wrong when Judas betrayed Him. That can certainly not be the case. There are some rebellions and betrayals that take place because the individuals concerned are intrinsically rebellious and demonically inspired. However, when a leader is out of God's plan, it opens the door for anarchy and disloyalty.

King Solomon is a perfect example of someone who experienced disloyalty because he deviated from God's plan. The Bible tells us that Solomon deviated from the will of God.

For it came to pass, when Solomon was old, that his wives turned away his heart after other gods: and his heart was not perfect with the Lord his God, as was

the heart of David his father. For Solomon went after
Ashtoreth the goddess of Zidonians, and after Milcom
the abomination of the Ammonites.

And Solomon did evil in the sight of the Lord, and
went not fully after the Lord, as did David his father.
Then did Solomon build an high place for Chemosh,
the abomination of Moab, in the hill that is before
Jerusalem, and for Molech, the abomination of the
children of Ammon. And likewise did he for all his
strange wives, which burnt incense and sacrificed unto
their gods. AND THE LORD WAS ANGRY WITH
SOLOMON...

1 Kings 11:4-9

As a result of Solomon's sins, the Bible explicitly tells us that
God raised up three rebels or enemies against Solomon. The first
one was Hadad, the Edomite.

For it came to pass, when Solomon was old, that his
wives turned away his heart after other gods: and his
heart was not perfect with the Lord his God, as was the
heart of David his father. And THE LORD STIRRED
UP AN ADVERSARY unto Solomon, Hadad the
Edomite: he was of the king's seed in Edom.

1 Kings 11:4, 14

The second traitor to the cause of Solomon was a man called
Rezon. He was an enemy to Israel all through the days of
Solomon. Apart from what Hadad the Edomite did, this man
Rezon was a pain in the neck of Solomon.

And God stirred him up another adversary, Rezon the
son of Eliadah, which fled from his lord Hadadezer
king of Zobah:

1 Kings 11: 23

The third disloyal person was Jeroboam, the son of Nebat.

And Jeroboam the son of Nebat, an Ephrathite of
Zereda, Solomon's servant, whose mother's name was

Zeruah, a widow woman, even he lifted up his hand against the king.

1 Kings 11:26

This man Jeroboam received a prophecy from a prophet called Ahijah. This prophecy contributed greatly to the future division of Solomon's kingdom. The prophecy in question shows us *the divine element* in the rebellions that occur.

And it came to pass at that time when Jeroboam went out of Jerusalem, that the prophet Ahijah the Shilonite found him in the way; and he had clad himself with a new garment; and they two were alone in the field: And Ahijah caught the new garment that was on him, and rent it in twelve pieces: And he said to Jeroboam, Take thee ten pieces: for thus saith the Lord, the God of Israel, Behold, I WILL REND THE KINGDOM out of the hand of Solomon, and will give ten tribes to thee: (But he shall have one tribe for my servant David's sake, and for Jerusalem's sake, the city which I have chosen out of all the tribes of Israel:) Because that they have forsaken me, and have worshipped Ashtoreth the goddess of the Zidonians, Chemosh the god of the Moabites, and Milcom the god of the children Ammon, and have not walked in my ways, to do that which is right in mine eyes, and to keep my statutes and my judgments, as did David his father. Howbeit I WILL NOT TAKE THE WHOLE KINGDOM OUT OF HIS HAND: but I will make him prince all the days of his life for David my servant's sake, whom I chose, because he kept my commandments and my statutes:
But I will take the kingdom out of his son's hand, and will give it unto thee, even ten tribes. And unto his son will I give one tribe, that David my servant may have a light alway before me in Jerusalem, the city which I have chosen me to put my name there. And I will take thee, and thou shalt reign according to all that thy soul desireth, and shalt be king over Israel.

1 Kings 11:29-37

19

Once again, please do not misunderstand me. I am not saying that God is behind every case of disloyalty. But in this case, the Bible is very plain about the cause of the rebellion. Being loyal to God and to his instructions for you will lead to human beings being loyal to you.

When Jesus was betrayed by Judas, did it mean that He was out of the will of God? Certainly not! Jesus always did the will of the Father. There are two groups of ministries or businesses. There are companies with a high rate of disloyalty and there are companies with a very low incidence of disloyalty. There are churches with a high number of traitors and rebels. In some churches, there is a new rebel every month. But in other churches you would find a much lower incidence of disloyalty. It is very unlikely to find a church with a one hundred percent level of loyalty.

4. Disloyalty Breeds Disloyalty

And Ahab called Obadiah, which was the governor of his house. (Now Obadiah feared the Lord greatly: For it was so, when Jezebel cut off the prophets of the Lord, that Obadiah took an hundred prophets, and hid them by fifty in a cave and fed them with bread and water.) And Ahab said unto Obadiah, Go into the land, unto all fountains of water, and unto all brooks: peradventure we may find grass to save the horses and mules alive, that we lose not all the beasts. So they divided the land between them to pass throughout it: Ahab went one way by himself, and Obadiah went another way by himself.

1 Kings 18:3-6

Obadiah was the governor of the house of King Ahab (who hated prophets). This means that he was a very important person to the king. He was a trusted confidant. In our modern world, we may have called him a Chief of Staff. Yet unknown to Ahab, Obadiah was secretly feeding hundreds of prophets. He was probably using King Ahab's food to support these prophets who were the archenemies of King Ahab. Obviously, Obadiah did not believe in the policies of King Ahab. His heart was not with the king.

This is a very common occurrence. There are many people who work closely with their superiors but do not believe in them. They undermine them all the time! How can a person be so close, yet so disloyal? Can you believe that Ahab's money was being used to finance the very thing he hated? This happens when there are disloyal people in important positions.

Many important positions are filled with disloyal and traitorous people. I remember a photograph I saw in a museum dedicated to the memory of Ghana's first president, Kwame Nkrumah. In this picture, the President, Kwame Nkrumah, is surrounded by six or seven smartly dressed and smiling generals. The guide who took us around the museum pointed to that photograph in particular and said, "This was the president and these were his generals." Then he continued and singled out one of the generals and said, "This is General Kotoka, the one who helped to overthrow the president."

As I looked at the photograph, I marvelled! Here was the president with his most trusted and senior men. Little did he know that in a few months, some of these trusted generals would oust him from office. That is betrayal for you!

Obadiah, the one we read about in 1 Kings 18, was in a similar position. He did not believe in what Ahab was doing. His real allegiance was to Almighty God. Why? I believe that the fact that Ahab was a rebellious king who did not obey the Lord was a signal to everyone around that rebellion and disloyalty were acceptable. Disloyalty breeds disloyalty! As soon as the spirit of disloyalty is manifested from the top, it begins to filter downwards. When the overall leader does not care for God or his principles, this attitude is transmitted down the ranks.

When the leader shows disregard for his subordinates it sends a signal to everyone. Many of the coup d'états and rebellions in Africa have come from frustrated people who feel that the president does not really care for the country. Mutinous soldiers arise from the ranks and murder their senior officers and senior government officials because they feel that these people no longer care for the common man. In other words, they perceive that the Head of State and his cronies are no longer loyal to the masses and their plight. This is often a trigger for a rebellion.

I am in no way saying that coup d'états or rebellions are justified. I am just showing you how they happen.

In the classic story of Julius Caesar, there was a conspiracy by his right hand man, Brutus and Cassius to overthrow their emperor. Julius Caesar was regarded as a hard, unyielding and uncaring leader. When Caesar arrived in the senate an appeal was made to him. In the unfolding drama, Metellus asks for his brother's banishment to be repealed. But Caesar tells him not to beg. Brutus joins the appeal, kneeling at Caesar's feet, yet Caesar remains firm. Julius Caesar then compares himself to the sun, the unyielding star which does not move in the heavens.

> *I am constant as the northern star,*
> *Of whose true-fix'd and resting quality*
> *There is no fellow in the firmament...*

He goes on to describe how the world is furnished with different kinds of men. Some of these are unshakeable, unmoveable and able to hold their rank.

> *So in the world: tis furnished well with men...*
> *And men are flesh and blood, apprehensive.*
> *Yet in the number I do know but one*
> *That unassailable holds his rank*
> *Unshaked of motion.*
> *And that I am he*

Yes, Julius Caesar, there are times to be unbending and unyielding, but there are also times to be flexible and merciful. Perhaps this attitude contributed to Julius Caesar's success on the battlefield. But this attitude does not accommodate many people permanently.

As I have said, one of the laws of loyalty is that 'disloyalty breeds disloyalty'. A leader must be loyal to the people he leads. You must genuinely care for the people you lead. You must genuinely help them. Many leaders are virtually sociological vampires. They rip and rape the people they lead, leaving them destitute and worse off.

If you desire to build numerous shops, businesses, and branches of your church, remember to be loyal to your people. You must develop a system of fairness. People must feel and perceive that there is equity, fairness and justice in the system within which they work. If people are promoted based on the whims and fancies of a manager, surely you are creating an atmosphere for disloyalty. When people are not rewarded for faithfulness and hard work, you are sowing seeds of disloyalty. When people do not get jobs based on merit, the environment for disloyalty is being created.

I know a country in which you cannot get a contract unless you have certain political qualifications. How unfortunate! This only means that everybody on the other side of the divide will be bitter. They will look for an opportunity to revolt against an unfair and unjust system. Never forget this simple fact, disloyalty breeds more disloyalty.

5. Loyalty Has a Single Eye

The light of the body is the eye: if therefore thine eye be single, thy whole body shall be full of light. But if thine eye be evil, thy whole body shall be full of darkness. If therefore the light that is in thee be darkness, how great is that darkness!

No man can serve two masters: for either he will hate the one, and love the other; or else he will hold to the one, and despise the other. Ye cannot serve God and mammon.

Matthew 6:22-24

In this scripture, Jesus teaches about how the entire body is affected by the eye. He says that if you have a single eye, your whole body will be full of light (a good thing). It goes on to say that if your eye is evil, your body will be full of darkness. What does a single eye mean? A single eye speaks of seeing one thing! In other words, in every sphere of life your attention should be focused on only one thing. Jesus went on to explain that you cannot serve God and mammon. In other words, if you see both God and mammon as "gods" in your life, you will not prosper. You must be loyal to one or the other. Jesus taught us that you would end up loving one and hating the other.

Can I Have Two Churches?

Another example concerns your church. You cannot have your attention focused on two churches. You must have a single eye! If you want to be loyal to your church, you must be focused on one church and not on two. A husband cannot be loyal to his wife if he has two women in his view. Any man with two different women in his sights has a potential for disloyalty. Do not forget this important principle, 'loyalty has a single eye'. If you belong to a church, your allegiance must be to the pastor in charge. You cannot say that there are two or three captains whom you look up to. You must see one person as your pastor, and that is the senior pastor. Everyone else is assisting the senior pastor to do the work.

There are some people who belong to churches and say, "If it were not for this junior pastor I would not stay in this church."

What they are saying is that they do not believe in the senior pastor. The junior pastor is therefore the only reason why they are still around. If that junior pastor were to break away, this individual would obviously follow the rebellion.

No matter which organization you belong to, it is important that you understand where your allegiance belongs. If you work in a company, your allegiance is to the highest authority.

If something is going wrong in your department, because you have a single eye, you will show your loyalty to your ultimate employer. Your allegiance will not be divided.

6. Loyalty Demands the Right Attitude

There are some attitudes that do not lead to loyalty. A suspicious person cannot be a loyal person. If you suspect me of wrongdoing, how can you be loyal to me? If you suspect that there is a snake in the room, how can you relax on your chair? Many people are suspicious about churches and pastors because of things they have heard. There are those who have made it their duty to spread bad stories about the ministry of the Lord Jesus. Their mouths are full of poison. They have convincing tales of the bad deeds of almost every minister of the gospel. Why is this? It's because Satan knows that you will be blessed through these men of God.

A Mixture of Good and Bad Creates Confusion

When you see a man of God ministering in such an anointed way, you will become confused because of the background stories you may have heard about him. Your confusion will effectively cut you off from fully receiving from that man of God. A mixture of good and bad is confusing to anyone. Because you are confused, you cannot give your full commitment or allegiance to the man of God or to his ministry.

I have seen many confused people in my lifetime. I once had a rebellious pastor who went around saying bad things about me. He told many people that I was a thief. He made people think that our church was a cult. The people who heard him speak became confused. I could see the confusion all over their faces.

One day I called two of these confused members and I told them, "These are the facts of the matter. Decide for yourself! Do not be confused. " I continued, "However, if you are confused, I think it would be better for you to go away to a church where you have full trust in the ministers."

In the process of time, their confusion vanished and they became stable and loyal members. Today, we laugh about the days when they were confused. When I look back, I realize that a person's commitment is greatly affected when he is confused.

Seemeth it a small thing unto you to have eaten up the good pasture, but ye must tread down with your feet the residue of your pastures? And to have drunk of the deep waters, but ye must foul the residue with your feet? And as for my flock, they eat that which ye have trodden with your feet; and they drink that which ye have fouled with your feet.

Ezekiel 34:18, 19

In this Scripture, God is angry at sheep that drank from the waters but afterwards fouled it up so that no one else could drink from it. Let me explain this in very simple terms.

There is a clear pool or pond from which we all drink. That pool represents your church. Hundreds of people have drunk from that pool and have never had a problem. Then along comes a brother who decides that he does not want to drink from that pool anymore. Instead of simply moving away from that pond, he urinates into the pool, thereby fouling it up.

...to have drunk of the deep waters, but ye must FOUL THE RESIDUE...

Ezekiel 34:18

From that moment onwards, anyone who comes to that pool will notice something unusual about the water. The water has an unusual colour and a foul smell. They will become confused and suspicious about drinking from the pool. No one would like to drink water mixed with urine. (I know you wouldn't!)

The confusion and suspicion is because one wicked person, who benefited from the pool like everyone else, has contaminated it. This is what happens when politicians leave political parties. This is what happens when ministers leave churches. They say such evil things about the churches to which they belonged for many years. They 'drank the waters' of that ministry and were blessed by it many times. Yet today, they have only evil things to say about it.

People tend to take such people seriously because they seem to have 'inside information'. This is what leads to the confusion and the suspicion. If you are a Christian leader, deal with confusion and suspicion in your congregation. Explain in detail what is happening and what has happened. Information helps to dispel suspicion. Explanations are very good antidotes for confusion and suspicion. It is sometimes painful to have to talk about certain things but there are times when you have no choice. I must warn you that some people's confusion is simply not dispelled by any explanations.

7. Loyalty Does Not Join or Create Factions

In every society or group, there are always people who create divisions. There are natural differences amongst people in every nation. God is the one who makes these natural differences. However, there are some people who seem to have an "eye" for these differences. They seem to notice them, talk about them and make something big out of these differences.

There are always members who want to magnify the differences that exist between pastors. They want to say how they prefer one pastor to the other. They say; "this pastor is really anointed, or that one is really caring". Some say "I prefer to come to church when this pastor is preaching, because it is more powerful". There are people who want to bring out tribal differences. They seem to know which tribe everyone comes from. They want everyone to be conscious of the differences in tribes or colour.

> **For it hath been declared unto me of you, my brethren, by them which are of the house of Chloe, that there are contentions among you.**
>
> **1 Corinthians 1:11**

27

These people existed in the time of Apostle Paul. There were people who were magnifying the differences in the leadership styles of Paul and Apollos. Such people only created confusion in the church.

A loyal person does not create or join factions of the church. In Ghana, there are people who always notice that people from certain tribes are doing certain things. In the church, such people create groupings based on tribe. I remember one day, a member in my church had to be confronted by another. This young lady confronted a leader and said, "Why is it that you only follow-up converts from this particular tribe?" She said to her, "You are creating a tribal group within our ministry and it is wrong!"

You see, without even noticing, some people carve out groups and sub-communities within the larger church. A loyal person is not interested in creating or joining such a group. There are some people who see the church as black or white. There are others who don't seem to notice these differences. Decide to be colour-blind in the church. You will be surprised to find out that God is not an American. The Lord is not white or black. Jesus was not a Baptist or a Presbyterian. He was not even a Pentecostal.

One of the works of the flesh is the ability to create parties and groups within every united body. This is not a good thing! Decide that you will not allow yourself to be used as a pawn for creating divisions in your church. Even businesses are destroyed when all sorts of imagined differences are magnified and spoken about.

The acts of the sinful nature are obvious: sexual immorality, impurity and debauchery; idolatry and witchcraft; hatred, discord, jealousy, fits of rage, selfish ambition, dissensions, FACTIONS AND ENVY; drunkenness, orgies, and the like. I warn you, as I did before, that those who live like this will not inherit the kingdom of God.

Galatians 5:19-21 (NIV)

One of the works of the flesh you must avoid is creating factions and groupings within a united body.

8. The Root of Disloyalty Is Pride

ONLY BY PRIDE cometh contention...
                                        Proverbs 13:10

The rebellion and divisions that happen in churches are often a result of deep-seated pride. It is often out of a spirit of pride that rebellion take place. I want us to look closely at the rebellion of Korah.

Now Korah, the son of Izhar, the son of Kohath, the son of Levi, and Dathan and Abiram, the sons of Eliab, and On, the son of Peleth, sons of Reuben, took men: And THEY ROSE UP BEFORE MOSES, with certain of the children of Israel, two hundred and fifty princes of the assembly, famous in the congregation, men of renown: And they gathered themselves together against Moses and against Aaron, and said unto them, Ye take too much upon you, seeing all the congregation are holy, every one of them, and the Lord is among them: wherefore then lift ye up yourselves above the congregation of the Lord?

And Moses said unto Korah, Hear, I pray you, ye sons of Levi: Seemeth it but a small thing unto you, that the God of Israel hath separated you from the congregation of Israel, to bring you near to himself to do the service of the tabernacle of the Lord, and to stand before the congregation to minister unto them? And he hath brought thee near to him, and all thy brethren the sons of Levi with thee: and seek ye the priesthood also? For which cause both thou and all thy company are gathered together against the Lord: and what is Aaron, that ye murmur against him?

                                        Numbers 16:1-3, 8-11

Moses was leading the people of Israel. He was surprised to find a group of princes rising up to challenge his authority. First of all, there was a large group in favour of this uprising. Two hundred and fifty princes were involved! These were not ordinary people! The Bible says that they were famous and of great renown.

...two hundred and fifty PRINCES of the assembly, FAMOUS in the congregation, MEN OF RENOWN...

Numbers 16:2

Obviously, they felt important. It is when people feel important that they raise their heads in rebellion. One person asked his pastor, "Why did the senior pastor not come to visit me?" He continued, "Why did you take so long in coming to visit me?" He told the pastor, "Do you not know that I am important to this church?" This gentleman continued to effuse all sorts of disrespectful remarks. It is pride that makes people disloyal and rebellious. You only rebel against a person when you think you are 'as good as' he.

Korah's group told Moses, "Why do you make yourself different from us?" They felt that Moses should be equal to them. This is the spirit of an equalizer.

...wherefore then lift ye up yourselves above the congregation of the Lord?

Numbers 16:3

They had forgotten that it was Moses who led them out of Egypt with incredible signs and wonders. They had forgotten about the quaking mountain, the thunder and the fire. Rebellious people often forget whom they are dealing with.

One rebellious pastor wrote a letter to me rebuking me and warning me for not recognizing his call. He signed the letter as an apostle to the Body of Christ. This gentleman had forgotten how I had trained him in the ministry. That is why he was now calling himself an apostle and rebuking me.

Moses sent for Dathan and Abiram, leaders of the reform rebel movement. They sent a rude reply back to Moses, "We will not come!" They were saying, "Who do you think you are to call us? If you want to talk to us, you better come over yourself!"

And Moses sent to call Dathan and Abiram, the sons of Eliab: which said, WE WILL NOT COME UP:

Numbers 16:12

It is only a spirit of pride which makes people speak like this. They saw themselves as equal to Moses. No one is equal to anyone, God made us all different. Whether you like it or not, some people are ahead and some are behind. Whether it suits you or not, some people are above and some are below. God did not create everything the same.

I remember some years ago, I sent a messenger to call one defiant pastor for a meeting. When the minister I sent arrived at the home of this man, this insubordinate pastor asked my emissary, "How can he call me for a meeting at such a time?"

He continued, "Who does he think he is? I am not coming!"

My messenger was taken aback, "What are you saying? You are going to create a problem." This anarchistic pastor said, "I am not just going to create a problem, I am going to create a big problem!"

Obviously, this mutinous pastor who was breathing fire and rebellion had gone the way of Dathan and Abiram.

You see, dear friend, there is nothing new under the sun. Everything that is happening today has happened before. The future can be predicted by studying what has happened in the past.

But what is the fruit of rebellion? What happens to people who behave like this? Read it for yourself.

And Moses said, Hereby ye shall know that the Lord hath sent me to do all these works; for I have not done

them of mine own mind. **IF THESE MEN DIE THE COMMON DEATH of all men, or if they be visited after the visitation of all men; then the Lord hath not sent me.**

But if the Lord make a new thing, and the earth open her mouth, and swallow them up, with all that appertain unto them, and they go down quick into the pit; then ye shall understand that these men have provoked the Lord.

And it came to pass, as he had made an end of speaking all these words, that the ground clave asunder that was under them: And the earth opened her mouth, and swallowed them up, and their houses, and all the men that appertained unto Korah, and all their goods.

They, and all that appertained to them, went down alive into the pit, and the earth closed upon them: and they perished from among the congregation.

Numbers 16:28-33

The end of rebels is the same – execution! Please do not allow pride to lead you into rebellion and disloyalty. I know you are a great person. I know you are as good as all the others. But please take your time and do not fight a battle you cannot win!

Since pride leads to disloyalty, it is important to identify symptoms of pride when they do occur. Watch out for these symptoms of pride.

Symptoms of Pride

- Answering back
- General rudeness
- Refusing to come when called
- Feeling indispensable
- Mocking and laughing at leaders
- Feeling that I am as good as my senior
- Constant criticism

9. Loyalty Is an Integral Part of Your Character

Someone said faithfulness is the cornerstone of your character. I believe it is true that loyalty is an integral part of your character. Loyalty is not simply a set of rules you must obey. **It is a matter of developing an invisible quality, a certain style and character of doing things.** Loyalty must emanate from the heart. It must not just be the following of instructions.

Developing loyalty is like developing a culture. You need to develop a culture of loyalty in the group of people you associate with. If you run a business, develop a culture of loyalty. A culture runs deeper than the rulebooks and the charts. It goes deeper than many things you see on the surface. It is an unseen force that keeps the family together.

When an individual has a culture and a character of loyalty, there are many things that no longer need to be said. When new people join your company or church, they begin to "see" how to do things around here. They discover that the system is airtight and unfriendly to treachery and to traitors. When something is part of a culture, it happens repeatedly even without prompting.

Dear Managing Director, dear Pastor, I suggest that you devote much of your energy to the promotion and cultivation of the culture of loyalty. When your organization is averse to disloyal elements, you will be much better off. If you are in business you will make profit. If you are in church work, your church will grow, expansion will take place.

When disloyalty is an integral part of an individual's character, he often repeats this treacherous behaviour without provocation. You will see this in the life of Jeroboam, the king of Israel.

First of all, Jereboam rebelled against King Solomon. Then he rebelled against Rehoboam, the legitimate king of Israel. After that, he rebelled against God. Notice Jeroboam's rebellion against King Solomon:

And Jeroboam the son of Nebat, an Ephrathite of Zereda, Solomon's servant, whose mother's name was Zeruah, a widow woman, even he lifted up his hand against the king [Solomon].

I Kings 11:26

Years later, this same Jeroboam rebelled against King Rehoboam. The rebellious streak within him was manifesting as the years went by. This is what happens with people who move from church to church. They always find something wrong with the leadership.

So when all Israel saw that the king hearkened not unto them, the people answered the king, saying, What portion have we in David? neither have we inheritance in the son of Jesse: to your tents, O Israel: now see to thine own house, David. So Israel departed unto their tents. But as for the children of Israel which dwelt in the cities of Judah, Rehoboam reigned over them. Then king Rehoboam sent Adoram, who was over the tribute; and all Israel stoned him with stones, that he died. Therefore king Rehoboam made speed to get him up to his chariot, to flee to Jerusalem.

SO ISRAEL REBELLED AGAINST THE HOUSE OF DAVID unto this day. And it came to pass, when all Israel heard that JEROBOAM was come again, that they sent and called him unto the congregation, AND MADE HIM KING OVER ALL ISRAEL: there was none that followed the house of David, but the tribe of Judah only.

1 Kings 12:16-20

Once again, with the passage of time, Jeroboam rebelled painfully against the Lord. He is the one who set up altars in Bethel and Dan for the children of Israel. He made calves of gold and made people worship them. He was a terrible disappointment to the Lord.

Then Jeroboam built Shechem in mount Ephraim, and dwelt therein; and went out from thence, and built Penuel. AND JEROBOAM SAID IN HIS HEART,

NOW SHALL THE KINGDOM RETURN to the house of David: If this people go up to do sacrifice in the house of the Lord at Jerusalem, then shall the heart of this people turn again unto their lord, even unto Rehoboam king of Judah, and they shall kill me, and go again to Rehoboam king of Judah.

Whereupon the king took counsel, and made two calves of gold, and said unto them, It is too much for you to go up to Jerusalem: behold thy gods, O Israel, which brought thee up out of the land of Egypt. And he set the one in Bethel, and the other put he in Dan. And this thing became a sin: for the people went to worship before the one, even unto Dan.

1 Kings 12:25-30

He ordained priests out of the most unqualified men in Israel.

And he made an house of high places, and made priests of the lowest of the people, which were not of the sons of Levi.

1 Kings 12:31

This is the man whom God raised up to become the king of Israel when he was a nobody.

And it came to pass at that time when Jeroboam went out of Jerusalem, that the prophet Ahijah the Shilonite found him in the way; and he had clad himself with a new garment; and they two were alone in the field: And Ahijah caught the new garment that was on him, and rent it in twelve pieces: And he said to Jeroboam, Take thee ten pieces: for thus saith the Lord, the God of Israel, Behold, I will rend the kingdom out of the hand of Solomon, and will give ten tribes to thee:

(But he shall have one tribe for my servant David's sake, and for Jerusalem's sake, the city which I have chosen out of all the tribes of Israel:) Because that they have forsaken me, and have worshipped Ashtoreth the goddess of the Zidonians, Chemosh the god of the Moabites, and Milcom the god of the children of Ammon, and have not walked in my ways, to do that

which is right in mine eyes, and to keep my statutes and my judgments, as did David his father.

Howbeit I will not take the whole kingdom out of his hand: but I will make him prince all the days of his life for David my servant's sake, whom I chose, because he kept my commandments and my statutes: But I will take the kingdom out of his son's hand, and will give it unto thee, even ten tribes. And unto his son will I give one tribe, that David my servant may have a light always before me in Jerusalem, the city which I have chosen me to put my name there.

And I will take thee, and thou shalt reign according to all that thy soul desireth, and shalt be king over Israel. And it shall be, if thou wilt hearken unto all that I command thee, and wilt walk in my ways and do that is right in my sight to keep my statutes and my commandments, as David my servant did; that I will be with thee, and build thee a sure house, as I built for David, and will give Israel unto thee.

1 Kings 11:29-38

Watch rebels closely! Rebellion is an integral part of a person's behaviour. After Jeroboam rebelled against King Solomon, he turned around and rebelled against God. Disloyalty is an integral part of a person's character and culture. Because of this it takes time for a person to imbibe and assimilate the philosophy, tradition and culture of loyalty. However, when it is established it yields wonderful fruits.

As you read this book, you may discover that you have traits of disloyalty. You may find out that the spirit of rebellion is manifest through you from time to time. This is dangerous. Rid yourself today of every tendency to rebel and to be disloyal. It cannot be the case that everyone around you is evil. Rebels always have good reasons for the things they do. Evil men are always full of good excuses. Hearken to the voice of the Lord today and become a man of faithfulness and loyalty.

10. Familiarity Breeds Disloyalty

To be familiar means to be more friendly and informal than is acceptable. It is a condition that develops between you and someone you know well, see often and hear often. There is a common saying that familiarity breeds contempt. In other words, familiarity leads to a loss of respect. This is often true. I would like to go a step further and say that familiarity also breeds disloyalty.

When a person is often seen and heard, he is usually taken for granted. That is why guest ministers are often appreciated more than the resident pastors. This should not be the case! A resident pastor often does more to make a program successful than the visitor does. Visiting ministers are often seen as heroes. The reason for this is because of the lack of familiarity.

Familiarity leads to a loss of respect and reverence. With time, this can progress into disloyalty. When Jesus came on the scene, He was not received in His hometown because the people were too familiar with Him. They asked one another, "Is that not the carpenter's son? Did He not repair our broken wardrobes and beds? Is he not a mere carpenter whom we have seen in this village for the last thirty years? How can He say that He is the Son of God?"

Is not this the carpenter, the son of Mary, the brother of James, and Joses, and of Juda, and Simon? and are not his sisters here with us? And they were offended at him. But Jesus said unto them, A prophet is not without honour, but in his own country, and among his own kin, and in his own house.

Mark 6:3, 4

By this Scripture, Jesus was saying that a prophet has a lot of honour in places where he is not known or seen much. Where are you seen and heard often? The answer is obvious, in your own country, among your own relatives and in your own house. What was the result of familiarity in Jesus' ministry? Jesus was not able to minister powerfully.

**And he could there do no mighty work, save that he
laid his hands upon a few sick folk, and healed them.**

Mark 6:5

But I want you to see a more dangerous effect of
familiarity - disloyalty. I want you to see that familiarity breeds
contempt, which can lead to disloyalty.

**And Miriam and Aaron spake against Moses because
of the Ethiopian woman whom he had married: for
he had married an Ethiopian woman. And they said,
Hath the Lord indeed spoken only by Moses? hath he
not spoken also by us? And the Lord heard it. (Now
the man Moses was very meek, above all the men which
were upon the face of the earth.)**

Numbers 12:1-3

Miriam was Moses' sister. She probably knew him very well.
She was a relative and knew all about his weaknesses. Aaron
was also someone who was very close to Moses. It seems that
they took this closeness for granted. A disloyal person often finds
faults and criticizes his leaders. That is exactly what Miriam
and Aaron did! They turned their attention to Moses' marriage.
"Why did Moses marry an Ethiopian woman," they said. "He is
out of the will of God." They were also deceived by the fact that
God had used them before. They said, "Has God not spoken by
us?"

Familiarity makes you forget important spiritual principles.
Familiarity brings deception to Christian leaders. Familiarity
makes people think that they can destroy God's servants.
Familiarity makes people forget the past.

Miriam and Aaron were taken up by the deception that came
through familiarity and criticized one of the greatest men of God
that ever lived. This provoked the Lord and He spoke to them.

**And the Lord came down in the pillar of the cloud, and
stood in the door of the tabernacle, and called Aaron
and Miriam: and they both came forth. And he said,
Hear now my words: If there be a prophet among
you, I the Lord will make myself known unto him in a**

vision, and will speak unto him in a dream. My servant Moses is not so, who is faithful in all mine house. With him will I speak mouth to mouth, even apparently, and not in dark speeches; and the similitude of the Lord shall he behold: WHEREFORE THEN WERE YE NOT AFRAID TO SPEAK AGAINST MY SERVANT MOSES? And the anger of the Lord was kindled against them; and he departed.

Numbers 12:5-9

Be careful when you speak against God's anointed servant. When you see him through the eyes of familiarity, you may think that He is a mere man. You will forget all that the Lord has accomplished through him. This will make you lose your reverence and you may walk into error.

Some years ago, I heard a very surprising story. There was a great man of God who had established about six thousand churches. He had preached in over one hundred different nations of the world. God had used him greatly to establish a Bible school that had trained thousands of young men and women for the ministry. I personally know several graduates of this great man's Bible school. The graduates of this Bible school have established churches and ministries all over the world. At one point, it was said that seventy percent of ministers in Africa were either his products, or products of his products.

He was known for massive evangelistic campaigns in which many fantastic miracles occurred. I spoke to one young man who told me how this man of God had raised the dead before his very eyes. Surely, this should be enough to show that he was not an ordinary person.

He was a mighty man of God, anointed of the Holy Spirit. Yet, I heard of an argument that one of his associate pastors had had with him. This man of God dismissed the associate. The associate turned to him and said, "You need to be slapped! "You cannot get away with this all the time," he continued.

When I heard about this, I was taken aback. I thought to myself, "How could someone threaten to slap such a great man of God? Was he not afraid?"

...wherefore then WERE YE NOT AFRAID to speak against my servant Moses?

Numbers 12:8

You see, familiarity has a way of breaking down reverence, respect and fear. Once these natural barriers are removed, acts of disloyalty happen more easily.

And the cloud departed from off the tabernacle; and, behold, Miriam became leprous, white as snow: and Aaron looked upon Miriam, and, behold, she was leprous. And Aaron said unto Moses, Alas, my lord, I beseech thee, lay not the sin upon us, wherein we have done foolishly, and wherein we have sinned.

Numbers 12:10, 11

After the judgment had come on Miriam, Aaron realized that they had been foolish to think that they could correct Moses. What people don't realize is that no human being can really correct a man of God. It is God who called them and it is God who will judge them. If you do not agree with or believe in a man of God, just move away quietly and leave him to the Lord. I can assure you that it is foolishness to fight against the Lord's anointed. You may think you have a cause, but you will discover that you are fighting against God.

You will notice in this passage that the Lord did not even bring up the subject of Moses having an Ethiopian wife. He just punished Miriam for speaking against his servant. You must realize that there are some things that are beyond our scope. Some church members think that they are a kind of jury assessing the pastor all the time. This is interesting! Who appointed them as jurors? The Bible teaches that we should not go beyond our jurisdiction.

Lord, my heart is not haughty, nor mine eyes lofty: neither do I exercise myself in great matters, or in things too high for me.

Psalm 131:1

Chapter 3

Five Rules of Loyalty

1. No Matter What You Do, Some People Will Be Disloyal

No matter what you do, some people will become disloyal in the process of time – so pray that it will not be you! This is what a pastor friend of mine said and I agree wholeheartedly with him. Work on yourself so that you do not fall prey to the deceptions that lead to disloyalty.

> **Jesus answered them, Have not I chosen you twelve, and one of you is a devil? He spake of Judas Iscariot the son of Simon: for he it was that should betray him, being one of the twelve.**
>
> **John 6:70, 71**

Jesus asked a very important question, "Have I not chosen you?" Jesus chose Judas Himself. He had selected him from among many others. Before Jesus took His final decision as to who should be His apostles, He went up to a mountain and prayed all night. Many of us do not take such care when making important decisions.

> **And it came to pass in those days, that he went out into a mountain to pray, and CONTINUED ALL NIGHT IN PRAYER to God. And when it was day, he called unto him his disciples; and OF THEM HE CHOSE TWELVE, whom also he named apostles; Simon, (whom he also named Peter,) and Andrew his brother, James and John, Philip and Bartholomew, Matthew and Thomas, James the son of Alphaeus, and Simon called Zelotes, And Judas the brother of James, AND JUDAS ISCARIOT, WHICH WAS ALSO THE TRAITOR.**
>
> **Luke 6:12-16**

I want you to notice how much care Jesus took when He chose the apostles. Did you know that the apostles were chosen out of a larger group of disciples?

What else could He do to prevent betrayal and disloyalty? **What could go wrong when a leader as wise and as anointed as Jesus takes a decision?** What could go wrong when a leader spends so much time in prayer? And yet, something went very wrong! Three and a half years later Jesus was betrayed by one of these apostles.

If this happened to Jesus, it can happen to you! You are not greater than your master!

Remember the word that I said unto you, The servant is not greater than his lord. If they have persecuted me, they will also persecute you; if they have kept my saying, they will keep yours also.
John 15:20

No matter your leadership abilities or strategies, some disloyalty is virtually inevitable. One out of the twelve disciples was a traitor. This is why I say that disloyalty cannot be prevented per se. However, it can be minimized greatly.

A good leader should be conscious of this principle. When you know that someone from within may one day fight you, you will be more careful about how you conduct your affairs. It is a very sobering thought to think that a familiar friend you eat with could one day turn against you. Such people may take things you said out of context to misrepresent you. *They may re-describe events to give a wrong impression.*

Yea, mine own familiar friend, in whom I trusted, which did eat of my bread, hath lifted up his heel against me.
Psalm 41:9

When you are conscious of the fact that potential traitors are in your midst today, you conduct your affairs with even greater circumspection! When you are aware that there is bound to be a traitor, you make extra precautions to ensure that *you do not become that traitor!*

The Betrayal of Julius Caesar

Julius Caesar was Rome's most successful general. After returning from battle in Spain, Julius Caesar was given a rousing reception. The pomp of his reception made two leading senators, Caesar's old friend Brutus, and the envious Cassius, fear that Caesar would declare himself emperor. Caesar himself did not trust some of the people. He saw in them the *signs of disloyalty.*

> ***Julius Caesar said:*** *Let me have men about me that are fat; Sleek-headed men and such as sleep o' nights; Yond' CASSIUS HAS A LEAN AND HUNGRY LOOK; HE THINKS TOO MUCH: SUCH MEN ARE DANGEROUS.*

Brutus reluctantly joined Cassius and other conspirators in a plot to murder Caesar. Although Julius Caesar was warned by his wife Calphurnia not to step out of the house on that day, he refused to listen. His wife spoke of graves and horrible sights she had seen in the night. But Julius Caesar would have none of that. He said,

> ***Julius Caesar said:*** *What can be avoided whose end is purposed by the mighty gods? Yet Caesar shall go forth; for these predictions are to the world in general as to Caesar. Cowards die many times before their deaths; The valiant never taste of death but once. Of all the wonders that I yet have heard, it seems to me most strange that men should fear, seeing that death, a necessary end, will come when it will come.*

Julius Caesar attended the senate and was brutally assassinated. Julius Caesar did not know that his closest aides were plotting his death. He had several close friends and assistants. Everybody expects their closest friend to expose wrongdoers and conspirators. **A truly loyal person will save you by telling you what is going on behind your back.** When your closest aides fail to do this your demise is imminent. Your business could collapse. Your company could go bankrupt. Your factory could register losses.

Your church could split up!

When the conspirators attacked Julius Caesar, he was startled. But his greatest surprise was when he found Brutus to be part of the conspiracy.

He said, "ET TU, BRUTE?" (You too Brutus?)

When Julius Caesar realized that Brutus was part of the conspiracy, he knew that all was lost. He said those famous words, which meant that it was all over. If your associates and trusted friends turn against you in ministry, your dreams of growth and expansion often end. Your vision for a great business often ends at the feet of disloyal people.

Julius Caesar said, "Then fall, Caesar!" (Then it's all over)

2. Teaching Is Immunization against Disloyalty

Teaching cannot totally prevent disloyalty but can minimize it greatly. Teaching is like primary health care that seeks to tackle health issues from the preventive point of view.

In September 1978, the International Conference on Primary Health Care met in Alma-Ata, and defined primary health care nicely.

Primary health care includes at least: EDUCATION concerning prevailing health problems and the methods of preventing and controlling them;   PROMOTION OF FOOD SUPPLY and proper nutrition; an adequate supply of SAFE WATER and BASIC SANITATION; maternal and child health care, including family planning;   IMMUNIZATION against the major infectious diseases; prevention and CONTROL OF LOCALLY ENDEMIC DISEASES;   appropriate treatment of common diseases and injuries; and provision of essential drugs *(Caps mine)*.

Primary health care was to form an integral part of the country's health system and become the central function and main focus. Health workers have realized that the mainstay of successful medicine is in the preventive dimension. You will notice that primary health care involves providing education, safe water, basic sanitation, immunization and a reliable food supply. These things are very good at improving the health of the nation. These things are also much cheaper to provide than costly surgical treatments.

I have said all this to say that the Church must see the wisdom in preventing spiritual problems. We must rise up and provide a good supply of food and spiritual immunization. Spiritual immunization involves teaching directly and unambiguously against disloyalty, betrayal, rebellion and ingratitude. Some pastors do not like facing issues head on. Immunization is not an injection that generally treats all diseases. It is a direct attack on a specific disease with the intention of preventing it.

Primary health care has not eradicated all diseases because, it cannot. However, it has definitely reduced the incidence of certain diseases. It has improved the general health of many nations.

God has shown us the way to prevent the destruction of his church. Let us embrace the wisdom of God and it will take us forward. Let us teach faithfulness and loyalty until the deception of rebellion is eradicated.

3. Teachings on Loyalty Must Be Remembered in the Hour of Temptation

And the Lord said, Simon, Simon, behold, SATAN HATH DESIRED TO HAVE YOU, that he may sift you as wheat: But I have prayed for thee, that thy faith fail not: and when thou art converted, strengthen thy brethren. And he said unto him, Lord, I AM READY TO GO WITH THEE, BOTH INTO PRISON, AND TO DEATH. And he said, I tell thee, Peter, the cock shall not crow this day, before that thou shalt thrice deny that thou knowest me.

Luke 22:31-34

45

Like with all temptations, it is important to remember the things we have learnt when it really matters. I have heard people make profound declarations of commitment. That is exactly what Peter did.

But when it really mattered, Peter forgot all the things he had said. You must remember the things you say. You must remember the pronouncements you make both in public and in private. What use is a husband who says sweet words at his wedding reception but forgets them two years later? Of what use is a man who says on his wedding night, 'I will love you forever' but dumps you after seven years? Forever does not mean seven years! Forever means forever!

You must remember the letters you write. It is easy to write things and to make promises. But it seems we all have a tendency to forget what we have said in the past. Thank God, Peter had a second chance. Peter was the most vocal apostle.

Everyone remembered Peter's declarations. All four Gospels record this incident and that is significant. You must realize that the writers of the Gospel did not always record the same events. For instance, Matthew, Mark and Luke recorded practically the same healings. They all recorded the healing of the woman with the issue of blood. But John, the writer of the fourth Gospel, did not. John recorded a number of healings. But most of the healings he recorded, such as the noble man's son in John chapter four, the lame man at the pool of Bethesda in chapter five, the blind man in chapter nine and the raising of Lazarus from the dead in chapter eleven were not recorded by Matthew, Mark and Luke.

However, Matthew, Mark, Luke and John did remember the incident of Peter's betrayal vividly. That is why it is reported consistently in the four Gospels. People will remember you by the things you said. Be careful to remember your commitment in the hour of temptation. You must be loyal to your promises. You must be loyal to your own words and pronouncements. You must be loyal to your written words.

Many of the people who have been disloyal to me in life and in ministry, said many positive things to me in the past. They were often the most vocal in their expression of commitment. I remember the things they said to me as though it were yesterday. They truly encouraged me at that time. As the years have gone by, I have become a little unimpressed with what people say. Like Jesus, my attitude is more of wait and see. Let's see what you will say when things get rough. I pray for my children in the Lord that they will be stable and faithful to the end.

Then took they him, and led him, and brought him into the high priest's house. And Peter followed afar off. And when they had kindled a fire in the midst of the hall, and were set down together. Peter sat down among them. But a certain maid beheld him as he sat by the fire, and earnestly looked upon him, and said, This man was also with him.

And he denied him, saying, WOMAN, I KNOW HIM NOT. [First Denial] And after a little while another saw him, and said, Thou art also of them. And Peter said, MAN, I AM NOT. [Second Denial] And about the space of one hour after another confidently affirmed, saying, Of a truth this fellow also was with him: for he is a Galilaean. And Peter said, MAN, I KNOW NOT WHAT THOU SAYEST.

[Third Denial] And immediately, while he yet spake, the cock crew. And the Lord turned, and looked upon Peter. And Peter remembered the word of the Lord, how he said unto him, Before the cock crow, thou shalt deny me thrice. And Peter went out, and wept bitterly.

Luke 22:54-62

Be a man of honour. Stand by your words. If you said you would be faithful to the end, then do so. Be a woman of virtue. Do not be erratic, unpredictable and wavering. It is in the hour of temptation that you must remember your sweet words of commitment.

4. Your Loyalty Is First to Jesus Christ

For there stood by me this night the angel of God, WHOSE I AM, AND WHOM I SERVE.

Acts 27:23

The Apostle Paul in the midst of his crisis, announced to everyone that he belonged to God and that he served the Lord. This fact must be at the forefront of every minister's mind. You are the Lord's, you have been bought with a price and you are to serve only God. If you are a minister of God, your service must be to God and not to politics or any other such thing.

A politician once approached me and asked for my support for his party. I told him, "I have learnt a few lessons in my short life. I cannot support you or any other party per se. I am a pastor and not a politician. No one should try to turn me into a politician for his own gain. I cannot give my support to you just because you ask for it or because you claim to be a Christian." I encouraged him, "If you tow the line of truth, freedom and justice you will naturally gain the support of Christians. I cannot give myself and my church wholesale to any political group." I do not belong to any political group; I belong to God! I belong to God and I serve God!

...whose I am, and whom I serve,

Acts 27:23

5. A Loyal Person Does Not Destroy What He Builds

For if I build again the things which I destroyed, I make myself a transgressor.

Galatians 2:18

There are many destroyers in the church. Many years ago, a large programme was organized on the university campus with the aim of winning all the unbelievers to Christ. A great man of God was invited as the main speaker for this programme. The crowds gathered in the Great Hall of the university. There was an air of expectancy on campus. To our surprise, when this man of God preached, he lashed out at Charismatic Christians.

He made a mockery of prayer meetings that were being held in the botanical gardens of the university. He said, "Christians were roaring like lions." He commented that no one could meditate peacefully in the gardens because the Charismatics were *roaring like lions*. This generated peals of laughter from the assembled students.

He continued to emphasize that loud prayer in the gardens was superfluous and backward. The people who had prayed for the souls to be saved and for the programme were being ridiculed. Maybe he forgot that Jesus prayed with loud cries and tears.

During the days of Jesus' life on earth, he offered up PRAYERS AND PETITIONS WITH LOUD CRIES AND TEARS to the one who could save him from death, and he was heard...

Hebrews 5:7(NIV)

Very few people were saved in those meetings! How would unbelievers be attracted to Christ when the pastor was taunting and sneering at Christians? We cannot destroy what we are trying to build. There was no significant addition to the Body of Christ. The destructive words cancelled all the efforts to build. When pastors who claim to be called to the ministry deride and denigrate other ministers, I ask whether they are building or destroying the Body. **Choose whether you are a builder or destroyer and stay within your calling.**

The most wicked and destructive statements I have ever heard about the Body of Christ have come from pastors. Ministers spread reprehensible stories about each other. They ridicule one another privately and from their pulpits. They blacken the reputation of other ministers. Then on Sunday morning they mount their pulpits and try to build the Body they have destroyed during the week.

Do not break down somebody's house in order to build yours. You will only reap what you sow! Do not break down someone else's church in order to build yours. How do you destroy a church? With your mouth of course! Let us choose whether we are building or destroying.

Chapter 4

Six Principles of Loyalty

1. A Loyal Person Exposes Wrongdoers to the Leadership

It is reported commonly that there is fornication among you, and such fornication as is not so much as named among the Gentiles, that one should have his father's wife.

1 Corinthians 5:1

Wrongdoers abound in every sphere of life. Wrongdoers abound at business places. When the manager is away there are all sorts of people who do their own thing. They steal, cheat, under-invoice and over-invoice. The list is endless. Human beings have a way of stealing and cheating in almost every sphere of life. People are sent out to buy things and they return with inflated and unreal prices. If such dishonest people are not under direct supervision, you can imagine the numerous evils that they will carry out.

A Loyal Person Keeps an Eye on Everything!

One loyal person will keep an eye on all these people. Once people know that there is someone who is loyal to the boss, they will often change their behaviour. They know that that person will not withhold information. Such a person is worth a lot to the manager.

Loyal People Can Incur Hatred!

A truly loyal person does not mind what people think about him. He will expose every crooked activity to his superior. He is genuinely loyal to one person – the head. Loyalty is a sign of good character. However, a loyal person will sometimes incur the displeasure and hatred of the people he exposes. Remember the example of Joseph.

These are the generations of Jacob. Joseph, being seventeen years old, was feeding the flock with his brethren; and the lad was with the sons of Bilhah, and with the sons of Zilpah, his father's wives: AND JOSEPH BROUGHT UNTO HIS FATHER THEIR EVIL REPORT.

Genesis 37:2

Joseph, the son of Jacob, was loyal to his father. He did not care what his brothers thought about him. He constantly reported the evil deeds of his brothers to their father. That is loyalty. Loyalty had its price – the hatred of his brothers. Loyalty also had its rewards. Jacob developed a special affinity and love for Joseph in particular.

Now Israel loved Joseph more than all his children...

Genesis 37:3

Unfortunately, there are many managing directors, leaders, presidents and pastors who do not know the value of a loyal person. They do not reward that loyal person for his loyalty. They treat loyal people as ordinary people. But Jacob valued his loyal son. I believe in placing value on loyalty.

...and he made him a coat of many colours.

Genesis 37:3

Jacob made a coat of many colours for Joseph. What do you do for people who are loyal to you? We often get the impression that Jacob loved Joseph because he was the son of his old age. That is true! But by studying this story you will see how the loyalty of Joseph and the disloyalty of his brothers led to Jacob's special love for Joseph.

Dear leader, you will only discover your losses after the loyal people have left. As I watch other pastors and general overseers struggle with disloyal branch pastors, I am so grateful to God for the loyal people he has given to me.

You will make far more profit when you value a loyal person. Experience is good. Education and qualifications are great, but place a high premium on fidelity. **Value someone who brings you true reports of what goes on behind your back.**

I have been a leader for some time. I know that people put up their best behaviour when they see me. Because of my position, I see smiling faces and receive the warmest of greetings all the time. Sometimes these cheerful and supposedly nice people have been saying bad things about me. This happens to every leader. That is why I value my loyal people. They are to me like Joseph was to Jacob.

Betrayal is a very common occurrence in this world. It is one of the most popular themes in the writing of books and the making of films.

Dear leader, dear pastor; do not expect people to know how to behave. Many people do not know the implications of their actions. I have realized that many subordinates do not know the implications of withholding information. It is important to teach on the subject of loyalty. It is important to train people to report evil as the family of Chloe did in 1 Corinthians 1:11.

Teach your followers that they will be rewarded for loyalty as Joseph was rewarded with a coat of many colours.

2. A murmurer is a disloyal person

Do all things without murmurings and disputings:
Philippians 2:14

Murmuring is when a person speaks about issues in undertones. People murmur because they feel that they cannot openly voice their opinions. Someone said, "I am afraid to ask a question because if I do, I will be branded as disloyal." That is not correct! A loyal person is someone who asks a lot of questions. **A loyal person is someone who finds out what he needs to know.** It is the subtle scoffing attitude with which questions are sometimes asked that make a person appear disloyal. But in reality, a genuine seeker of information is not a disloyal person.

I encourage people to ask questions. In fact, I am more at ease with people who ask questions and make contributions. I feel very uneasy with people who have nothing to say or ask. It is not possible that you have no questions on your mind. God gave you a questioning and reasoning mind. Murmuring is an evil way of speaking.

A good leader must encourage questions and openness. Murmurers do not amount to much. They are discontented people with hearts of bitterness. The murmuring is just a manifestation of deep-seated feelings of hatred. I do not trust murmurers and neither does God.

And all the children of Israel MURMURED against Moses and against Aaron: and the whole congregation said unto them, Would God that we had died in the land of Egypt! or would God we had died in this wilderness! And wherefore hath the Lord brought us unto this land, to fall by the sword, that our wives and our children should be a prey? were it not better for us to return into Egypt? And they said one to another, Let us make a captain, and let us return into Egypt. And the Lord said unto Moses, How long will this people provoke me? And how long will it be ere they believe me, for all the signs which I have shewed among them?
Numbers 14:2-4, 11

The children of Israel murmured against Moses on several occasions. Murmuring is often a product of fear. Loyalty is not compatible with fear. The Bible says: "fear has torment" and "perfect love casts out fear". It is likely that the children of Israel were afraid of Moses because of the spectacular signs and wonders that were associated with him.

There is no need to fear your leader. Be open and honest with him. Because the children of Israel did not approach Moses openly, they resorted to murmuring and that brought a curse upon them. Murmuring is like an evil spirit. The Bible teaches us not to murmur as the children of Israel murmured. Every disloyal person will be destroyed. Disloyalty manifests itself through murmuring.

Neither murmur ye, as some of them also murmured, and were destroyed of the destroyer.

1 Corinthians 10:10

Murmuring is a spirit. If you are a leader, watch closely for people who are always mumbling and whispering to each other. They speak to each other under their breath. When you ask them what they are talking about they say, "Oh, nothing much."

Dear leaders, when people murmur, they are usually talking about you. Murmuring is like a cancer that doesn't go away. You must get rid of all the murmurers in your group. It destroys the person and those around him. Gradually, that spirit pollutes everyone around. I can tell you very plainly that I do not trust people who complain, murmur and speak under their breath. Notice God's reaction to complaining and murmuring people.

And when the people complained, it DISPLEASED the Lord: and the Lord heard it; and his ANGER was kindled and the FIRE of the Lord burnt among them, and CONSUMED THEM...

Numbers 11:1

3. Disloyalty is the fruit of ignorance

A loyal person must study history. In order to be loyal to a cause you need to be fully persuaded about the vision. Loyalty demands full persuasion. The Apostle Paul wrote to Timothy because certain people were criticising Paul to Timothy. In order to encourage Timothy, Paul asked him to remember nine different things about his (Paul's) life and ministry. Paul made this personal reference because it had become necessary to reassure Timothy.

But thou hast fully known my doctrine, manner of life, purpose, faith, longsuffering, charity, patience, Persecutions, afflictions, which came unto me at

Antioch, at Iconium, at Lystra; what persecutions I endured: but out of them all the Lord delivered me.
2 Timothy 3:10, 11

Before you can fully believe in a vision, you must study the doctrine, the lifestyle, the purpose and the faith of the people concerned. Paul reminded Timothy of his longsuffering, charity, patience, persecutions and afflictions. It is important to know about the problems someone has had in the past. Why did the person have those difficulties? Was he at fault? Did he do something wrong? Was he persecuted out of jealousy? Are the stories about him true or false?

Some people have had persecutions because of sins and mistakes they have made. Others have had problems because they were doing the right thing.

Before you join a new church or ministry, it is important to delve into the historical background of that ministry. Many people follow false religions without studying the history of that group. If they were to study the history of their leaders, they would never support or believe in them. If however you were to study the life of Jesus Christ, you would discover that he was a noble and righteous man. He was truly without blemish. However, the same cannot be said about some other people. Jesus was murdered on the cross not because he had siphoned away a nation's wealth, but because he was paying for the sins of the world.

Even though our Lord Jesus suffered a humiliating death on the cross, it was not because he had done anything wrong. Jesus Christ never raided and looted towns. Jesus Christ did not marry ten different women. Jesus Christ did not marry children. Yet he suffered many things and was murdered by the people of his day.

When Peter preached that famous sermon about the name of Jesus, he told the Pharisees, "I know you. You killed Jesus." He knew the history of the town. He knew why and how Jesus died.

Then Peter, filled with the Holy Ghost, said unto them,
Ye rulers of the people, and elders of Israel, If we this

day be examined of the good deed done to the impotent man, by what means he is made whole;Be it known unto you all, and to all the people of Israel, that by the name of Jesus Christ of Nazareth, whom ye crucified, whom God raised from the dead, even by him doth this man stand here before you whole.

Acts 4:8-10

Instead of rushing to believe in something without fully understanding it, delve into its historical background.

Elisha Knew the History!

When Elisha began his ministry, he was called upon to minister to the king. Was Elisha supposed to flow with this backslidden king or not? Was he supposed to cooperate with this secular leader? There seemed to be no apparent reason why not! Elisha had had no previous interaction with this king. He was a new prophet and the king was also newly appointed.

But Elisha said something that showed he was fully aware of all that had gone on in the past. He told king Jehoram, "If it was not because I respected King Jehoshaphat I would not even lift up my head in your direction." He went on to say, "If my eyes were even to fall in your direction, I would not see you." This is a very strong statement to make to a king.

And Elisha said unto the king of Israel, What have I to do with thee? GET THEE TO THE PROPHETS OF THY FATHER, AND TO THE PROPHETS OF THY MOTHER. And the king of Israel said unto him, Nay: for the Lord hath called these three kings together, to deliver them into the hand of Moab. And Elisha said, As the Lord of hosts liveth, before whom I stand, surely, were it not that I regard the presence of Jehoshaphat the king of Judah, I would not look toward thee, nor see thee.

2 Kings 3:13, 14

Elisha was being very uncooperative because of the historical background of the king. This king was the person whose father

57

had hunted down his 'father', Elijah. He had hunted him down like an animal. Ahab had served other gods and worshipped idols. Because Elisha was a student of church history, he knew that he could not flow with such a person. He told the king to seek help from his father's prophets!

Loyalty demands full persuasion in all areas. When I studied the background and the history of Christianity and Jesus Christ, I became more convinced about the faith that I had found. Indeed, a general study of history will help you greatly to develop loyalty in the right direction.

4. Disloyalty is the fruit of immaturity

I have realized that many people become disloyal because they are not mature in the things of God. When Absalom broke away from the regular army and attacked his father, many people followed him. But that is not all! The Word of God describes the state of their minds. It says that they were simplistic. It says that they were simple people and they did not know much.

And with Absalom went two hundred men out of Jerusalem, that were called; and they went in their SIMPLICITY, and THEY KNEW NOT ANYTHING.
2 Samuel 15:11

You see, if you really understand what you are doing you may not go ahead with rebellion. That is why I preach and teach on disloyalty. The more we teach on this subject, the more awareness is created. It is not a good thing to be a Judas, an Absalom or Lucifer. These are bad names you should not be associated with. Who would really like to be a rebel when all rebels end up being executed?

Mild and Serious Disloyalty

In the ministry of Jesus, it was not only Judas who betrayed Christ. Peter also betrayed Christ. He swore and cursed that he did not know Jesus. Was this not a betrayal? If you got into trouble and needed help, would you not be disappointed if your friend said he did not know you? Would you not feel that he had betrayed you in your time of trouble? I know you would! But this is exactly what Peter did.

Yet, it is not only Peter who deserted Christ at the moment when he needed support. The other disciples were nowhere to be found. They all abandoned ship when it was most critical. That is betrayal! Yet, Christ did not put them in the same category as Judas. Judas was manifesting what I call serious disloyalty and the other disciples were manifesting mild disloyalty.

Characteristics of Serious Disloyalty

• **In serious disloyalty the rebel concerned actually engineers an uprising, demonstration or revolt against authority.**

You will notice that the disciples did not engineer anything; they were victims of the circumstances.

• **In serious disloyalty, the traitor is often disloyal for monetary gains.**

• **Seriously disloyal people will sacrifice their friends for any flimsy reason.**

• **Seriously disloyal people lie about you with the intention of hurting or destroying you.**

They spread evil stories about the person in order to destroy him. Notice that the disciples did not spread any bad stories about Christ after they had deserted him.

• **Serious disloyalty, (e.g. Lucifer, Absalom or Judas) is usually untreatable, not correctable and without remedy.**

Characteristic of Mild Disloyalty

• **In mild disloyalty, you will notice features of betrayal and desertion and abandonment.**

- **Such people are usually caught up by the events of the day.**

The disciples were caught up by the momentous events of the night.

- **They do not personally engineer or create a rebellion against authority.**

Neither do they help to destroy the church or business.

- **Mildly disloyal people follow wrong things out of simplicity.**

They do not understand the issues at stake. Many people follow things only to find out that they have made a mistake. I have had people leave the church only to return and apologize profusely for their mistake.

> **And with Absalom went two hundred men out of Jerusalem, that were called; and THEY WENT IN THEIR SIMPLICITY, and THEY KNEW NOT ANY THING.**
>
> **2 Samuel 15:11**

- **Mildly disloyal people are often confused by events.**

They don't know what is right or wrong and they don't understand what is happening. To them, the pastors in the church are in conflict and they wish it would all end happily

- **Mildly disloyal people often act in fear and ignorance.**

They are frightened by conflicts. They do not know anything about rebellion or insurgencies.

- **Mild disloyalty can often be remedied with time.**

- **Mild disloyalty often manifests itself as confusion and uncertainty.**

Whenever there is a shake-up in a church, such people are often caught in the middle of the fight. They don't know who is right and who is wrong. You cannot really blame them as they don't really know what is going on.

And Jesus saith unto them, All ye shall be offended because of me this night: for it is written, I will smite the shepherd, and the sheep shall be scattered. But after that I am risen, I will go before you into Galilee. But Peter said unto him, Although all shall be offended, yet will not I.

And Jesus saith unto him, Verily I say unto thee, That this day, even in this night, before the cock crow twice, thou shalt deny me thrice. But he spake the more vehemently, If I should die with thee, I will not deny thee in any wise. Likewise also said they all.

Mark 14:27-31

Even though Jesus' disciples were not loyal to Him when it really mattered, I believe that He considered it to be a result of immaturity. Because of this I often overlook things that people say, knowing that they will come to understand. Often a person is critical because he is inexperienced. Sometimes assistant pastors are critical of the senior pastor because they have never been head pastors before. If you are a senior pastor, it is important to check this before it grows into a serious rebellion.

The School of Hard Knocks

One of the best ways to deal with mild disloyalty is to allow the individual to go through certain experiences himself. If your associate pastor feels that you are not a good head pastor, one of the best things to do is to send him to the 'school of hard knocks'. Allow him to be a senior minister. Let him pioneer a church. He will mature in no time! The 'school of hard knocks' issues certificates of maturity. You will also receive a diploma in understanding from this 'school'.

As he pastors a church himself and has people under him, he will begin to appreciate the responsibilities and pressures that come upon a leader. There are some people who are not able to appreciate these realities without experiencing head-ship themselves. However, some ministers have the grace to assist without going through this 'school'.

After the disciples had abandoned Jesus, you will notice that He did not rebuke them for betraying Him. Jesus understood them! Jesus knew that it was a stage of development and gave them another chance. He just said to them, "Go into the world and preach the gospel." Jesus was sending the disciples in to the 'school of hard knocks'. When you read the letters of Peter, you will realise that he met various rebellious people in his ministry. He learnt first-hand about loyalty.

When you give people a chance, they often turn out very well. The disciples became so loyal to Christ that many of them died for their faith. Those who fled in the early days of their ministry had matured into faithful diehard loyalists. To die for someone is the highest form of commitment you can ever have. Many people experiencing mild disloyalty can turn around to become the most loyal people you could ever have.

5. Loyalty today does not mean loyalty tomorrow

The fact that you are faithful today does not mean that you will be faithful tomorrow. A Christian needs to be loyal because the devil does not go on vacation. Jesus overcame the devil in the wilderness. The Bible teaches us that the devil went away for a season and not forever. The devil will leave you for a while but not forever.

And when the devil had ended all the temptation, he departed from him for a season.

Luke 4:13

At different times in the history of King David's reign, he had sons who tried to usurp his authority and take the throne. The first time it happened, a young man named Absalom was involved in the conspiracy.

And there came a messenger to David, saying, The hearts of the men of Israel are after Absalom. And David said unto all his servants that were with him at Jerusalem, Arise, and let us flee; for we shall not else escape from Absalom: make speed to depart, lest he overtake us suddenly, and bring evil upon us, and smite the city with the edge of the sword.

2 Samuel 15:13, 14

In this particular instance, Joab, David's army commander, was loyal and fought against Absalom. He was so zealous that he even killed Absalom when David was crying for mercy for his son. This was a great display of loyalty to the cause of the King.

And Absalom met the servants of David. And Absalom rode upon a mule, and the mule went under the thick boughs of a great oak, and his head caught hold of the oak, and he was taken up between the heaven and the earth; and the mule that was under him went away. And a certain man saw it, and told Joab, and said, Behold, I saw Absalom hanged in an oak. Then said Joab, I may not tarry thus with thee. And he took three darts in his hand, and thrust them through the heart of Absalom, while he was yet alive in the midst of the oak.

2 Samuel 18:9, 10, 14

However, several years later another son of David, named Adonijah, tried to take the throne. This time Joab was not loyal to David. It was exactly the same situation that had happened a few years earlier with Absalom. Another child who had no business on the throne, wanted to become the king. Please read the following Scripture carefully.

Then ADONIJAH the son of Haggith EXALTED HIMSELF, SAYING, I WILL BE KING: and he prepared him chariots and horsemen, and fifty men to run before him... and his mother bare him after Absalom.

And HE CONFERRED WITH JOAB the son of Zeruiah, and with Abiathar the priest: and THEY FOLLOWED ADONIJAH AND HELPED HIM.

1 Kings 1:5-7

Notice how Joab, who had fought against Abasalom a few years earlier was now helping Adonijah. Is it not ironic that someone who was once loyal to David could become disloyal?

I remember a brother who was so loyal to me. He would stand up at meetings and declare his commitment each time. He was noted for his proclamations and utterances about his commitment to me. One day, at a meeting, we were discussing the actions of a rebellious pastor. This gentleman stood up and condemned the behaviour of this rebel. As I listened to him, I was encouraged by his words of commitment and support. I said to myself, "I really have some loyal people with me." Sometime later this brother was appointed a pastor and pioneered a church somewhere. It was not but a few years later when this pastor rebelled against me in a very surprising move.

One afternoon he said to me, "I would like to see you." I said, "Sure, I'm always here. You can see me now." He started, "I have decided to begin a new church." "Which church is this," I asked. "A church," he replied. "Is it part of Lighthouse Chapel?" I asked. "No," he answered. "Oh, I see!"

This was his way of telling me that he was pulling out unexpectedly. Shortly after, in an unanticipated move, he changed the name of the Lighthouse church he was pastoring and retained some of our properties. This person had been very loyal to me for several years. It was a surprise to almost everyone! His loyalty to me was convincing and impressive! But this illustrates the principle. *Loyalty today does not mean loyalty tomorrow.*

Joab was loyal in the case of Absolam but not in the case of Adonijah. We must therefore be vigilant so that we do not fall prey to the attacks of the enemy in the future.

Nowadays, I take speeches and proclamations of commitment with a pinch of salt. I pray for people who make statements of commitment, that as the years go by they will remember what they have said and live by it.

6. Only loyal people catch the anointing

Loyalty has its rewards. No one can forget that statement. "Well done, good and faithful servant." We will be rewarded for our faithfulness to God.

> **...Well done, thou good and faithful servant...**
> **Matthew 25:21**

You will also be rewarded for your faithfulness to the men you serve. Jesus said, "Whosoever receiveth you, receiveth me."

> **Verily, verily, I say unto you, He that receiveth whomsoever I send receiveth me; and he that receiveth me receiveth him that sent me.**
> **John 13:20**

When you are loyal to your pastor / boss, God considers it to be faithfulness to him. As I said in an earlier chapter, loyalty is an integral part of your character. If you are faithful to man, you are likely to be faithful to God. Loyalty pays off! It will cost you to be disloyal!

Many people think of Elisha as Elijah's servant. But what you must realize is that Elijah had two servants. No one even knows the name of the first servant. It was the first servant of Elijah who saw most of the great miracles! Do you remember the story of how Elijah prayed for rain? You will remember that Elijah kept sending his servant to see if there were any clouds on the horizon. That was the first servant.

> **And Elijah said unto Ahab, Get thee up, eat and drink; for there is a sound of abundance of rain. So Ahab went up to eat and to drink. And Elijah went up to the top of Carmel; and he cast himself down upon the earth, and put his face between his knees. AND SAID TO HIS SERVANT, Go up now, look toward the sea.**

And he went up, and looked, and said, There is nothing. And he said, GO AGAIN seven times.

And it came to pass at the seventh time, that he said, Behold, there ariseth a little cloud out of the sea, like a man's hand. And he said, GO UP, SAY UNTO AHAB, Prepare thy chariot, and get thee down, that the rain stop thee not.

And it came to pass in the mean while, that the heaven was black with clouds and wind, and there was a great rain. And Ahab rode, and went to Jezreel. And the hand of the Lord was on Elijah; and he girded up his loins, and ran before Ahab to the entrance of Jezreel.

1 Kings 18:41-46

This man saw Elijah call down fire from Heaven. This man saw Elijah challenge the false prophets of Ahab. Elisha never saw these things, he just read about them. Later on, Elijah got into trouble with Jezebel because of his powerful ministry against the false prophets.

And Ahab told Jezebel all that Elijah had done, and withal how he had slain all the prophets with the sword. Then Jezebel sent a messenger unto Elijah, saying, So let the gods do to me, and more also, if I make not thy life as the life of one of them by to morrow about this time.

1 Kings 19:1, 2

Elijah was terrified and decided to flee for his very life. It was at this point that his first servant left him.

And when he saw that, he arose and went for his life, and came to Beersheba, which belongeth to Judah, AND LEFT HIS SERVANT THERE.

1 Kings 19:3

Whether Elijah asked his servant to wait behind or his servant abandoned him for fear of his life, no one knows. Whatever the case, *this servant did not stay till the end.* This is the last we hear of him. How sad! This man could have been the next anointed prophet of the Lord. Perhaps his name would have filled several chapters of the Bible.

When Elijah got to Mount Horeb the Lord spoke to him about several things. One of the things was about getting a new servant to replace the old guy who had left him. This is how Elisha came to replace the first servant!

...and Elisha the son of Shaphat of Abelmeholah shall thou anoint to be prophet in thy room.

1 Kings 19:16

I often wonder why people do not stay till the end where they will receive all that God has for them. God has a great calling for many of us. We need an anointing to fulfil that call. It is by staying to the end that we catch the anointing. Most of the great blessings come at the end of the race. No one gets a medal for starting a race. The medals are for those who finish the race!

In the Christian world, many ministers are like university students who did one or two years of study, but never completed their courses. You see, many people think that they have arrived after they become familiar with the ministry. Familiarity with pastors and with the church is not the same as experience in ministry. Some people think that the ministry is as easy as that. Many people do not know that it takes years of faithful following and loyalty!

As I go on in the ministry, I realize that there are many things that I do not know. No one knows it all. It is said that Elisha followed Elijah for twenty years before he received the anointing.

It is important to learn from the mistakes of your predecessors. I think that is exactly what Elisha did, and it paid off! In the last days of his ministry, Elijah tried to leave Elisha in the same way he did to the first servant.

And it came to pass, when the Lord would take up Elijah into heaven by a whirlwind, that Elijah went

**with Elisha from Gilgal. And Elijah said unto Elisha,
Tarry here, I pray thee; for the Lord hath sent me to
Bethel. And Elisha said unto him, As the Lord liveth,
and as thy soul liveth, I WILL NOT LEAVE THEE. So
they went down to Bethel.**

2 Kings 2:1, 2

Elijah tried four times to get rid of his servant Elisha. He was
going to have an experience with God and he didn't want anyone
to be around. But Elisha was not to be moved. Elijah looked at
Elisha in the face and said, "I have a new vision. I am moving
on without you!" I think Elisha remembered what happened to
the first servant and he decided to be faithful to the end. Elisha
replied, "Your vision is my vision."

Once again, Elijah tried to get rid of Elisha at Bethel. But
Elisha would have none of it. He had decided to stay till the very
end. He knew that **loyal people receive the anointing.** Elijah
told Elisha, "The Lord has sent me." Elijah did not say, "The
Lord has sent us." He said, "The Lord has sent me."

Elisha just looked at Elijah and said blandly, "The Lord has
also sent me to that same place!"

When they got to Jericho, Elijah said, "God has sent me
to Jordan. Please go back home. There is no place for you
anymore."

**And Elijah said unto him, Tarry, I pray thee, here: for
the Lord hath sent me to Jordan. And he said, As the
Lord liveth, and as thy soul liveth, I will not leave thee.
And they two went on.**

2 Kings 2:6

In other words, Elijah told Elisha, "I have a new dream.
God has spoken to me and I must go on without you. I'm off to
Jordan!" But Elisha knew what was at stake and simply replied,
"Your dream is my dream. *Whatever you want to do is what I
want to do!*" In the end, Elisha was an eyewitness to that precious
experience of Elijah being caught up into Heaven.

Many people think that Elijah was taken into Heaven by a chariot of fire. The chariot and horses of fire were used to separate Elijah and Elisha and not to take Elijah to Heaven. Elijah was taken up to Heaven by a whirlwind and not a chariot.

And it came to pass, as they still went on, and talked, that, behold, there appeared a chariot of fire, and horses of fire, and parted them both asunder; and Elijah went up by a whirlwind into heaven.

2 Kings 2:11

Elisha was so glued to his mentor and pastor that it took a supernatural force to separate them. This is a lesson to us all. A loyal person catches the anointing. **Elisha became doubly anointed after this experience.** Elijah did sixteen miracles but Elisha did thirty-two miracles. Elijah promised that a double anointing would be on Elisha if he were loyal to the very end (when he was taken away).

And it came to pass, when they were gone over, that Elijah said unto Elisha, Ask what I shall do for thee, before I be taken away from thee. And Elisha said, I pray thee, let a double portion of thy spirit be upon me. And he said thou hast asked a hard thing: nevertheless, IF THOU SEE ME WHEN I AM TAKEN from thee, it shall be so unto thee; but if not, it shall not be so.

2 Kings 2:9, 10

Dear friend, never forget this important fact about loyalty. God will bless you because of your faithfulness, loyalty and fidelity. Your loyalty will earn you the anointing. You may even receive a double portion!

Chapter 5

Three Causes of Disloyalty

In this chapter, we want to examine three common causes that lead a person to disloyalty. The first thing we will consider is what I call an erratic personality or character.

1. An Erratic Personality

There are some people who have a disposition to make sudden decisions. They can alter the plan of their lives within minutes. They can change their entire course within seconds. This is a very dangerous trait. Such people can be with you today but can desert you tomorrow.

You will notice this trait in people who enter relationships and break up suddenly. When they speak of their commitment to a cause, you will be impressed by their speech. But don't be fooled! These people are usually gifted speakers and orators. They will change direction without any major provocation, to your surprise!

I am not writing about some theory in the Bible. I am talking about practical things that I have seen. **I have seen the most committed and ardent followers change course in midstream.** Because I have seen several people do this, I am convinced that it is a character or personality trait which some people have.

This is what the Bible speaks of in Proverbs 24:21.

My son, fear thou the Lord and the king: and meddle not with them that are GIVEN TO CHANGE:
Proverbs 24:21

Do you have a tendency to change course suddenly after you have been extremely committed to something? I would not like to be in a relationship like that! I would not like to have an assistant pastor like that. Such people will write letters to you when you are not expecting them. They will resign at the weekend without notice. They will ask someone to phone you to tell you that they are out of the country.

Their word is not worth anything! A Christian must be a person who makes a statement and sticks to his word no matter what it costs.

...He that sweareth to his own hurt, and changeth not.
Psalm 15:4

God is faithful to us even when we are not faithful to Him. Nothing makes Him change His mind!

If we believe not, yet he abideth faithful: HE CANNOT DENY HIMSELF.
2 Timothy 2:13

God is trying to build up a breed of Christians who do not change their minds easily about the convictions they have. Thank God that Jesus did not change His mind when He came into this world and experienced such hatred and animosity from the people He loved.

The ministry of the Lord Jesus Christ is not safe in the hands of erratic leaders. Today, they are ministers of the gospel and tomorrow they become social activists. Some switch suddenly from being ministers of religion to becoming politicians. Today, they are faith preachers and tomorrow they are against the faith movement!

You will often notice a trend in the lives of such people. There is a history of changing, altering and switching from one thing to the other. If you have an erratic nature, decide today to be a solid and steadfast believer.

2. Financial Reasons

The next cause of disloyalty has financial roots.

For the love of money is THE ROOT OF ALL EVIL: which while some coveted after, they have erred from

the faith, and pierced themselves through with many sorrows.

1 Timothy 6:10

The love of money is the root of all evil. Certainly, one of the evils that is stirred up by the love of money is disloyalty and rebellion. I have noticed that almost every rebellion is linked to some financial considerations. There is something about money that stirs up disloyalty. There are two categories of problems that arise from financial roots – financial misunderstanding and financial covetousness.

Financial Misunderstanding

Many of the rebellions in denominations are over issues of salaries, conditions of services, emoluments and benefits. There is often a background of financial need and poverty. **I have seen many Christians serve the Lord perfectly, but they seem to change when financial issues come up.** There are several reasons why money causes problems and leads to divisions in churches.

Firstly, many pastors have not had any working experience in the secular world and therefore, they have unfortunate misconceptions about how much they should be paid. They do not know what kinds of salaries and benefits prevail.

One day, I attended a seminar for leaders in another church. At one point in the meeting, there was a general discussion about the conditions of service for ministers. I began asking some questions.

I called out three people and asked them, "How long have you been working?" One of them had been working for sixteen years in a bank. The other had worked as a teacher for eight years. The third had been into private business for several years. Then I asked them, "Which of you has a car?" None of them owned a car! You see, in the economy of Ghana you almost need to be a millionaire to own a car. I then pointed out some things to the group. "Look at this man who has worked in the bank for sixteen years. His workplace has not provided him with a car." I continued, "Do you see this teacher who has taught for eight years and yet has no car?" "The businessman who controls his own income has not been able to buy a car." I asked the group, "Why is it that when someone becomes a pastor, he wants to be given a car immediately?"

I pointed out that the educational qualifications of many of the pastors are very minimal. In the secular field, many of these pastors could not rise higher than the position of a security officer or a clerk. Yet, they want to have conditions of service similar to Chief Executives! This is just not realistic.

Indeed, this common misunderstanding between junior pastors and senior pastors of the management rank is a common cause for rebellion, discontentment and anarchy in churches.

Anarchism is a political theory that all governments and laws should be abolished. It comes from a French word, 'anarchy'. An anarchist is someone who fights governments. When such a person becomes a pastor, you can imagine the controversy and conflict he will stir up. He will try to dismantle the order and authority structure in the church. He will say things like, "We are all equal! We are all called! We are all anointed! We will not allow ourselves to be cheated by anyone!"

Because of this common misunderstanding that arises between the employer and the employed, I am very careful about employing anyone. I have very few employed staff. I believe that people must mature in their understanding of employment issues. If we are not careful, the church can turn into another forum for unions and strikes! Soon there may be industrial action taken against bishops and head pastors.

One thing I do not like, is to work with discontented people. I learnt that from the Lord. Do you remember how the Lord abandoned the Israelites in the desert because they complained so much? There was so much murmuring among the Israelites that Almighty God was fed up. He took a decision to relieve them of their privileged position!

Once I had some full-time pastors working in a church. They began to complain about their conditions of service. Soon I received different reports of various comments they had made. It sounded as though the church was mistreating them. I marvelled because these young men did not appreciate what they had.

As the intensity of the complaints mounted, I decided to lay them off. I would rather not have a church than to have a church with a complaining pastor. We called them to the headquarters and gave them a handsome amount of money to settle them. I heard that they even complained about the amount of money that was given in the settlement. I told them, "Look for jobs in the secular world and be lay pastors."

They began to look for jobs in the secular world. After several months one of them returned and said, "I now realize that I had one of the best jobs in Ghana." He pleaded to be re-employed by the church. This is the maturing experience I am referring to.

If you are an overseer of a group of churches, I would advise you to allow discontented people to discover for themselves what conditions prevail out there in the hard world. It is important that you maintain an atmosphere of loyalty at all costs.

Financial Covetousness

When I speak about covetousness I am not talking about people who are in need. In this case, we are dealing with people who want more, more and more! The Bible teaches that people who love money are not satisfied with more money.

He that loveth silver shall not be satisfied with silver...
Ecclesiastes 5:10

Apostle Peter warned against people who enter the ministry for the love of money. The ministry is the wrong profession if all you want is to acquire wealth. If you love money, please stay in the secular world and earn all you can. When you come into the ministry, your aim must be to make full proof of your calling. God's ministry is not a business so please do not turn it into one.

Do you remember how Jesus threw out people who turned the church into a business centre?

And they come to Jerusalem: and Jesus went into the temple, and began to cast out them that sold and bought in the temple, and overthrew the tables of the moneychangers, and the seats of them that sold doves; And he would not suffer that any man should carry any vessel through the temple. And he taught, saying unto them, Is it not written, My house shall be called of all nations the house of prayer? but YE HAVE MADE IT A DEN OF THIEVES.

Mark 11:15-17

I cannot leave this subject without mentioning two classic examples of pastors who suffered from covetousness (Rev. Gehazi and Rev. Judas!). Gehazi, the associate pastor of Elisha could not resist the temptation of using the ministry as a business. He wanted to charge money for the gift of God. He was charging for prophecies and healings. Does that sound familiar?

Naaman the Syrian, the one whom he charged, detected the spirit of covetousness in Rev. Gehazi. Why do I say that Naaman detected the spirit of covetousness in Gehazi? Because, even though Gehazi asked for one talent of silver, Naaman, the unbeliever, said to him, "Be content and TAKE TWO talents." Naaman detected the pastor's spirit of greed!

And Naaman said, BE CONTENT, TAKE TWO TALENTS. And he urged him, and bound two talents of silver in two bags, with two changes of garments, and laid them upon two of his servants; and they bare them before him.

2 Kings 5:23

It is sad that an unbeliever should have to correct a minister of the gospel in this way. Gehazi was virtually told by a sinner not to be greedy. Dear pastor, did you know that unbelievers can see through our greed and covetousness?

They laugh at us in their homes and denigrate the ministry of the Lord Jesus Christ (to denigrate means to blacken the reputation of a thing). It is unfortunate that when you call yourself a minister today, people look at you with suspicion. This is because of Rev. Gehazi and others like him.

Elisha, the senior pastor, asked a very pertinent question.

...IS IT A TIME TO RECEIVE MONEY, and to receive garments, and olive yards and vineyards and sheep and oxen and men servants and maid servants?

2 Kings 5:26

The ministry of the Lord Jesus is not the place to make money. Neither is it the time of your life to gather wealth. I am not saying that God will not make you wealthy! I am not saying that you should be poor! I am not poor and I have not taken a vow of poverty. God will bless you with all you need so that you can serve Him, but this will be at the right time!

Judas Iscariot sold his master for only thirty pieces of silver. The current value of thirty pieces of silver is $19.20!

And said unto them, What will ye give me, and I will deliver him unto you? And they covenanted with him for thirty pieces of silver.

Matthew 26:15

Incidentally, that was the price of a slave.

If the ox shall push [kill] a manservant or a maidservant; he shall give unto their master thirty shekels of silver, and the ox shall be stoned.

Exodus 21:32

Rev. Dr. Judas Iscariot lost his life and ministry because of greed and covetousness. Twenty US dollars is all that it took to make him sacrifice his friend, his master and his God. **He sold *God* for twelve pounds sterling, (twenty Euros, thirty Swiss francs, fifty Ghanaian cedis)!**

If you ever employ a Judas or a Gehazi, you are in for trouble. They will never be satisfied with what you offer them. They will always think you are cheating them. They will try to usurp your authority and take over. Such people can easily be taken away by someone who offers them more money.

3. Missing God's Direction

The third common cause of disloyalty, is missing God's direction for your life.

Many people miss God's direction for their lives. Because of this, they end up in complicated situations. They are often forced into disloyalty by their own mistakes. Every minister must know how to hear the voice of God. The leading of the Spirit is crucial for successful ministry.

Many ministers claim that they are being led by the Spirit of God as they breakaway and rebel in the ministry. Are these people really being led by the Spirit of God? Many people are having what I call visions of their own heart.

> **...The prophets PROPHESY LIES in my name: I sent them not, neither have I commanded them, neither spake unto them: they prophesy unto you a false vision and divination, and a thing of nought, and THE DECEIT OF THEIR HEART.**
> **Jeremiah 14:14**

> **Thus saith the Lord of hosts, Hearken not unto the words of the prophets that prophesy unto you: they make you vain: they speak A VISION OF THEIR OWN HEART, and not out of the mouth of the Lord.**
> **Jeremiah 23:16**

A common trick of people who go their own way is to claim that God has sent them. The scripture tells us that we should not listen to the words of such prophets. When someone has a rebellious spirit, he will surely dream about a successful rebellion. God says in his Word; I sent them not, neither have I commanded them, neither spake unto them: they prophesy unto you a false vision and *the deceit of their hearts (Jeremiah 14:14).*

A Scriptural Rebellion?

I watched a junior pastor as he rebelled against his senior pastor. His mouth was full of venom. He went about slandering his former church and criticizing his former pastor. Yet this man had scriptures to back his claim. He claimed that God had called him and asked him to do what he was doing.

I said to this rebel, "God does not destroy churches! God is a builder of churches."

He was my friend so I went with him to the new church he had established. When I got there, I realized that all the equipment he was using belonged to his former church. He had taken over the church's seats, pulpit and instruments. He had their members and their building. I said to him, "These things do not belong to you." I continued, "It is stealing." He just smiled and said, "You don't understand." I continued, "You are my friend, but God's blessing will not be with you when you do such things." Within a few years, this anarchist's ministry collapsed!

If even an angel appears to you and gives you instructions, we will not accept it if it is contrary to the Word of God! The Bible teaches us not to believe when people speak a vision out of their hearts. How can God in one stroke build a church and in the next stroke destroy it?

Anyone who goes around slandering other ministers is a dangerous person. **Snakes are not discriminating when they begin to bite.** After spreading venom about someone else, they will turn on you.

I know a pastor who abandoned ship because a prophet told him to. Later on, I found out that this same prophet would send scouts to the church in which he was going to minister. These scouts would take car numbers and descriptions and find out who the owners were. The prophet would use this information to conjure up "words of knowledge". These words of knowledge were so spectacular and astonishingly accurate that everyone believed the prophet's word.

Finally, he had a prophecy for the associate pastor, "This is not your place. You must begin your own church." You cannot imagine the confusion that broke out in that church. The visit of this prophet changed the course of that ministry. The church broke up into many splinter groups. The pastors ended up fighting in court over church property.

The Bible says that we shall know them by their fruits. I would not criticize anybody for his accurate words of knowledge. I pray for accurate words of knowledge myself and I am happy when I see them happening. The Bible did not teach me that I would know a thing by its gift. You know them by their fruits.

When I see the fruits of broken churches, destroyed ministries and deceived pastors, I know that the Spirit of God is not at work. The devil and the flesh are on the rampage.

But if ye have bitter envying and strife in your hearts, glory not, and lie not against the truth. THIS WISDOM DESCENDETH NOT FROM ABOVE, BUT IS EARTHLY, SENSUAL, DEVILISH. For where envying and strife is, there is confusion and every evil work.

James 3:14-16

Dear minister friend, do not yield to pressure from people. You may make the mistake of your lifetime. People will push you into things but they will not support you when you are out there. Somebody once told me, "people sympathize with the underdog, but they follow the top dog".

When I first got married, people often suggested the number of children that we should have. Some said we should have five, others said we should have four children. They would describe the advantages of having large families. "How nice it is when they all grow up and you have children all over the world," they said. "You can have such nice family reunions. The children will have lots of playmates."

I would smile to myself and think, "This man is suggesting that I have all these children. Will he look after them when they grow up? Will he pay their school fees and build houses for them? Certainly not!" Those who will not contribute a dime are those who put the most pressure on you!

Dear friend, be careful about yielding to the pressure of the people. When you have taken the wrong decision, these same people will criticize you for making mistakes.

Judas came under pressure to betray Christ. He eventually succumbed to the pressure and temptation to betray his master. Afterwards, he realized that he had made a mistake. He went back to these same people who had pressurized him with money and made a lame attempt to undo everything. He actually took the money back! **But the people would have none of it and threw him out to face suicide and eternal damnation *on his own.*** They told Judas, "What is that to us? That is your problem! See to it yourself!"

Then Judas, which had betrayed him, when he saw that he was condemned, repented himself, and brought again the thirty pieces of silver to the chief priests and elders, Saying, I have sinned in that I have betrayed the innocent blood. And they said, WHAT IS THAT TO US? SEE THOU TO THAT. And he cast down the pieces of silver in the temple, and departed, and went and hanged himself.

Matthew 27:3-5

Please do not yield to the temptation of money or to the pressure of the people. You will have to deal with the consequences of your decisions by yourself!

Chapter 6

The Timing of Disloyalty

When I write about disloyalty, I am writing about a whole array of things. These range from subtle acts of disloyalty to betrayals, insurgencies and open rebellions.

But, when do these things happen? Do they happen all the time? Or do they have specific seasons and timings? A close study of the Bible will reveal that acts of disloyalty are more common at particular times. In this chapter, we will study what I call the timing of disloyalty. Let us now consider four important times when disloyalty may occur.

1. Disloyalty occurs with the apparent weakening of a leader.

All leaders go through different phases of their lives and ministries. In the prime of their ministry, they often appear very strong, hard, tireless and invincible. Leaders may appear to weaken in the latter part of their ministries. They seem to be vulnerable to things that before were far off. This apparent weakening of a minister is not actually a diminishing of his strength. Sometimes in later years, the maturing minister speaks with a softer tone and is more accommodating. Sometimes it is a result of entering into another phase of ministry.

In the early part of Jesus' ministry, He was very strong on certain things. At one point He spoke about how He was anointed and people tried to kill Him. At that stage of His ministry Jesus just ignored His persecutors and went His way.

And all they in the synagogue, when they heard these things, were filled with wrath, And rose up, and thrust him out of the city, and led him unto the brow of the hill whereon their city was built, that they might cast him down headlong. But he passing through the midst of them went his way.

Luke 4:28-30

At one point, Jesus preached and called His listeners snakes. He told them to their face that they were vipers.

O generation of vipers, how can ye, being evil, speak good things?

Matthew 12:34

Jesus was a strong direct preacher. He was a no-nonsense personality. There was a time when people wanted to kill Him. Jesus told them directly, "I know you want to kill me." He continued, "Your father is the devil." These were direct statements which infuriated the crowd. Yet, Jesus persisted in this line of confrontational preaching.

But now ye seek to kill me, A MAN THAT HATH TOLD YOU THE TRUTH, which I have heard of God: this did not Abraham. Ye do the deeds of your father. Then said they to him, We be not born of fornication; we have one Father, even God. YE ARE OF YOUR FATHER THE DEVIL, and the lusts of your father ye will do. He was a murderer from the beginning, and abode not in the truth, because there is no truth in him.

When he speaketh a lie, he speaketh of his own: for he is a liar, and the father of it. Then took they up stones to cast at him: but Jesus hid himself, and went out of the temple, GOING THROUGH THE MIDST OF THEM, AND SO PASSED BY.

John 8:40, 41, 44, 59

In those days, Jesus did not seem to be moved by death threats. But later in his life, Jesus began to say things like, "I am going to suffer!"

And he said unto them, With desire I have desired to eat this passover with you BEFORE I SUFFER...

Luke 22:15

At another point, Jesus was in a reflective mood and said, "This is my last drink."

82

For I say unto you, I will not drink of the fruit of the vine, until the kingdom of God shall come.

Luke 22:18

Jesus continued and said, "There is a betrayer amongst us." If He was a good leader, why didn't He do anything about the betrayer. Had He lost His power? Judas must have heard these words and felt that Jesus' power was waning.

Jesus' power never diminished. The anointing on His life was stronger than ever. If His power had diminished, how come He was able to heal the boy whose ear was cut off by Peter (John 18:10)? If His power was diminished, how come everyone fell under the power of God when Jesus identified Himself as the one they were looking for?

As soon then as he had said unto them, I am he, they went backward, and fell to the ground.

John 18:6

Jesus' power had in no way diminished, but He had entered a different phase of His ministry. This power would help Him go to the cross and accomplish his sacrifice for the sins of the world. But Judas misinterpreted this to be a weakening of His master's anointing. Judas was encouraged to rise up and rebel against the Lord when He heard Him speak of dying. If you eat with someone who speaks of dying and taking His last drink, would you not think there was something wrong?

The High Priest and the Pharisees were afraid of Jesus. There was great mystery and intrigue surrounding Christ! Jesus was a public figure and they could have arrested Him at any time. Jesus did not go around in secret. But they feared the people and were unsure of what sort of powers Jesus would conjure up against them if they tried anything.

Judas waited for a sign of the apparent weakening of Christ's ministry. As soon as he felt his leader was a little weaker, he betrayed Him. Dear pastor, do not be deceived. If God has called somebody, and you betray Him, you will pay for it! It may seem easy to rebel at certain times, but that is the devil luring you to your own destruction.

2. Disloyalty occurs with the aging of the leader.

For it came to pass, when Solomon was old, that his wives turned away his heart after other gods: and his heart was not perfect with the Lord his God, as was the heart of David his father.

1 Kings 11:4

King Solomon turned away from God in his old age. It may sound strange, but it sometimes requires physical strength to keep on doing what is right. King Solomon had married so many different women in his younger days. He wanted to be sure that he did not fall into the mistake of adultery as his father did. So he married all the ladies he met to prevent himself from having an affair with anyone. But in his old age, the resolve to serve Jehovah was weakened. He began to succumb to the pressures of his 'unbeliever' wives.

Then did Solomon build an high place for Chemosh, the abomination of Moab, in the hill that is before Jerusalem, and for Molech, the abomination of the children of Ammon. And likewise did he for all his strange wives, which burnt incense and sacrificed unto their gods.

1 Kings 11:7, 8

I am a young man. As I write this book it is my prayer that I will be loyal to the Lord as I get older in ministry.

In the life of King David, it was when he was very old and stricken in years, that Adonijah rebelled against his father. Adonijah was one of David's sons who had been a loyal member of the family for many years. He did not rebel with Absalom. Nor was he associated with any other rebellion. Yet, he was tempted to be disloyal when he realized that his father was weakened by old age.

Now king DAVID WAS OLD and stricken in years; and they covered him with clothes, but he gat no

heat. THEN ADONIJAH THE SON OF HAGGITH EXALTED HIMSELF, saying, I will be king: and he prepared him chariots and horsemen, and fifty men to run before him.

1 Kings 1:1, 5

3. Disloyalty occurs when the leader sins.

When Solomon went after many wives and his heart was turned against God, the Lord raised up rebels to fight against him.

And the Lord was angry with Solomon, because his heart was turned from the Lord God of Israel, which had appeared unto him twice, And the Lord stirred up an adversary unto Solomon, Hadad the Edomite: he was of the king's seed in Edom.

1 Kings 11:9, 14

It is the grace of God that keeps a church together. What prevents one person from rising against another? It is the mercy of the Lord. What prevents a bodyguard from shooting his own leader in order to become famous? It is the grace of God.

A leader must be aware that God's mercy upholds all things. You will not have a single loyal person with you unless God helps you. Ladies and gentlemen, the power of the presidency and the power of leadership are maintained by a delicate balance of forces. God's grace is what sustains us in all our endeavours. We may give many teachings about disloyalty and loyalty. We may print all the books we can on the subject. Ultimately, it is the grace of God that holds all things together.

Jehoshaphat was a famous king of Judah. He served the Lord and God wrought miracles under his regime. God gave the Israelites more blessings than they could carry under the reign of Jehoshaphat. When Jehoshaphat died his son Jehoram took over. Jehoram was not like his father and became associated with Ahab the evil king of Israel. This is because he married the daughter of Ahab.

It is interesting to note that under the reign of this backslidden king, a group of people who had lived in submission to Judah for many years rebelled. The Bible tells us clearly that the people of Edom became disloyal and traitorous under the rule of Jehoram. But why did they stay submissive under Jehoshaphat?

> **...JEHORAM the son of Jehoshaphat king of Judah began to reign. And he walked in the way of the kings of Israel, as did the house of Ahab: for the daughter of Ahab was his wife: and he did evil in the sight of the Lord. IN HIS DAYS EDOM REVOLTED from under the hand of Judah, and made a king over themselves.**
>
> **2 Kings 8:16, 18, 20**

It is clear from this Scripture that the timing of the revolt of Edom was related to the type of king in Judah. The revolt took place under the hand of an evil person. Acts of disloyalty by followers are often related to acts of disobedience by leaders.

4. Disloyalty occurs upon the death of a leader.

I have watched many churches disintegrate after the death of their founders and leaders. Why does this happen? **Disloyal people are often looking for an opportunity to break away or revolt against authority.** They are opportunists who will grab at any sign of weakness within the system. Often the death of a leader signifies to them the removal of a factor that has long prevented them from rebelling.

Recently in one African country, the dictatorial head of state died. When his assistant took over, he pursued policies completely opposite to what his leader did. He freed all the enemies of his former boss and set about to return the country to a democracy – something his predecessor was opposed to. What does this mean? It showed that the assistant was not loyal to the former head of state's ideologies. He could not say or show it publicly whilst his boss was alive. However, upon the death of his leader, his true feelings were manifested! This is a very common occurrence in life.

I remember when a great founder and leader of a denomination in Ghana died. It was not long before some of the prominent pastors of his denomination separated themselves. I also recall when a founder of a great denomination in Nigeria died. It was but a few months before some of the most prominent ministers disassociated themselves from the church. **Rebellious people sense a weakening in the system by the passing away of the leader.**

The unexpected death of a head of state can cause instability in a nation where the power is already held in delicate balance. In some countries, the head of state does not even have to die. All he has to do is to travel outside the country. Kwame Nkrumah, the first president of Ghana, was overthrown in a coup d'état when he travelled outside Ghana for a short while. He was in Hanoi for a meeting when he was overthrown. He was never to return to Ghana in his lifetime.

Some pastors are afraid to travel away from their churches because of this.

Ahab, the king of Israel, was a wicked but strong ruler. He had the Moabites under control. But when he died, Moab rebelled almost immediately.

And Mesha king of Moab was a sheep master, and rendered unto the king of Israel a hundred thousand lambs, and an hundred thousand rams with the wool. But it came to pass, WHEN AHAB WAS DEAD, THAT THE KING OF MOAB REBELLED against the king of Israel.

2 Kings 3:4, 5

This is a common pattern for revolts. You see, there are many people who are rebels at heart but are afraid to make a move. They are watching for a sign, a change, a weakening or an opening. With little provocation they will separate themselves and fight against the authorities.

Are you a rebel at heart? Will your loyalty persist even when there is an apparent weakening of the leader? Will age, sin or even death of your leader turn you into a rebel? Time will tell!

87

Chapter 7

Six Manifestations of Disloyalty

To manifest means "to 'demonstrate', to 'display', 'exhibit' or to 'show forth'" something. People show disloyalty in many ways. In this chapter, I want us to study a few of the common manifestations of disloyalty.

Why do we need to look at the manifestations of disloyalty? Because loyalty and disloyalty are things of the heart and things of the heart cannot easily be seen. Like many diseases, it is best detected by watching out for symptoms.

Let us now look for these important symptoms and signs of disloyalty.

1. Disobedience

The first important manifestation of disloyalty is disobedience. Disobedience is an outward manifestation of a disloyal heart. Watch out for disobedient people, they are probably disloyal at heart. God disposed of Saul after he disobeyed him.

And Samuel said, Hath the Lord as great delight in burnt offerings and sacrifices, as in obeying the voice of the Lord? Behold, to obey is better than sacrifice, and to hearken than the fat of rams. For rebellion is as the sin of witchcraft, and stubbornness is as iniquity and idolatry. Because thou hast rejected the word of the Lord, he hath also rejected thee from being king.
1 Samuel 15:22, 23

Disobedient people often have a rebellious streak. It is the spirit of rebellion that gives them the audacity to disobey.

2. Scorning

Blessed is the man that walketh not in the counsel of the ungodly, nor standeth in the way of sinners, nor sitteth in the SEAT OF THE SCORNFUL.

Psalm 1:1

Scorners are people who mock at you. They do not believe in you or in what you are doing. The Bible very clearly tells us that we must not associate with scoffers. According to Psalm 1:1, we are not even supposed to sit in the same chair with the scornful. How can somebody who does not believe in you be your assistant pastor? How can someone who despises you be an associate to you?

Yet, this is a situation existing in many churches today. The scornful are sitting in the same chair with you. Can you understand why your ministry is not blessed? The Bible says; blessed is the man who sitteth not in the seat of the scornful. **Blessed is the pastor who does not sit next to a scornful assistant.**

What must you do with a scornful person? Should you pray about the scoffers? Should you fast for a week? The answer is NO! There is a biblical remedy for dealing with scornful people.

CAST OUT THE SCORNER, and contention shall go out; yea strife and reproach shall cease.

Proverbs 22:10

According to Proverbs 22:10, the biblical remedy for dealing with scoffers is to cast them out! In modern English, to cast out means: to dismiss, to expel, to eject, to banish, to fire, to sack, to discard, to unseat or to lay off. If you are wiser than God, you can pray about it. If you know more than God, you can handle scornful people in your own way. I prefer to trust the wisdom of God. I will dismiss, expel, eject, banish, fire, sack, discard, unseat and lay off any scoffer in my set-up. That is the biblical way to deal with disloyal people!

3. Inflexibility

Inflexibility is a manifestation of disloyalty. An inflexible person is stubborn and defiant. **Watch out for inflexible people in your set-up.** Such people do not want to work overtime. They do not want to go beyond what is stipulated in their contract. They are not prepared to adapt to any new situation. They will always point out to you that work ends at 5.00 p.m.! They are unwilling to do anything extra for the organisation. Woe to the manager if he asks them to do something new! A sulking face is the trademark of such inflexible workers.

Inflexible church members are not prepared to stay on if the church service goes beyond the stipulated time. An inflexible and unyielding person is difficult to work with. He can become disloyal to you when things no longer suit him.

Stubborn people are also not prepared to take correction when they are confronted. You will see this in the life of Saul. When Samuel confronted him about the war with the Amalekites, he argued with Samuel. He was inflexible and unyielding in his discussion with Saul. He insisted that he had obeyed the Lord. The evidence of his disobedience was obvious and yet Saul argued with Samuel.

> **And Samuel came to Saul: and said Saul unto him, Blessed be thou of the Lord: I HAVE PERFORMED the commandment of the Lord. And Samuel said, WHAT MEANETH THEN THIS BLEATING of the sheep in mine ears...**
>
> **1 Samuel 15:13, 14**

Some years ago, I had a worker who misused some church property. Initially, he denied everything! Because of this, I collected a lot of documentary evidence to prove that he was actually misappropriating the equipment and the church's money.

When I had gathered all the documents, I called for a meeting. I presented all the documents that showed unambiguously that this gentleman had disobeyed instructions. Would you believe that in spite of the evidence in black and white, this man argued with us for three hours? I watched as an inflexible and unyielding attitude was flagrantly displayed. I said to myself, "How stubborn can a person be?" Indeed, it was only a matter of time before this stubborn individual became openly rebellious. Truly, stubbornness is a manifestation of disloyalty!

4. Lies

I am convinced that if demons could have twins, then the twin of the spirit of lying would be the spirit of stealing. Lying and stealing always go together. Anybody who lies to you is not loyal to you. His heart cannot be with you.

Watch out for liars, they are very dangerous people! Do you know how to catch a liar? Let me share with you a little secret I use. Listen to people as they speak casually. When they jokingly tell you about how they lied to someone and got away with it, take note! Since he is capable of lying effortlessly to other people, he can do the same to you.

I believe that truth is an integral part of your character. If the belt of truth is absent, you are exposed to demons. If God hates a lying tongue, it must be the duty of every Christian, leader or manager to hate the same thing.

These six things doth the Lord hate: yea, seven are an abomination unto him: A proud look, a LYING TONGUE, and hands that shed innocent blood,
Proverbs 6:16, 17

Liars are disloyal people!

5. Tale-bearing

…and he that soweth discord among brethren.
Proverbs 6:19

There are people who have the ability to create stories and recreate events to suit themselves. They can spread stories and make things sound interesting. Have you noticed that newspapers often have tragic or scandalous events as their headlines? Bad news is sweeter to the gossips than good news.

Watch out for people who have endless tales about others. They know every bad event that has occurred in the church. They are ready to give you a complete rundown on any story you request. They know the details and they have inside information. Watch out for such people. They sow discord and division within the camp.

6. Rudeness

And Moses sent to call Dathan and Abiram, the sons of Eliab: which said, WE WILL NOT COME UP...

Numbers 16:12

Dathan and Abiram were openly rude to Moses. They refused to come when he called for them. Most people express their animosity behind the backs of their superiors. People who lash out at you openly with their tongues can lash out at you in other ways.

Rudeness is a manifestation of disloyalty. Watch out for it!

Chapter 8

The Loyalty of Christ

Many of us do not realise how loyal Jesus was to his Father in Heaven. He exhibited this many times. He made many statements that teach us great truths about loyalty. In this chapter, I want us to learn the principles of fidelity, loyalty and faithfulness directly from Jesus Christ.

Perhaps all that you know about Jesus are the miracles that he performed. But Jesus is the express image of God and if we want to learn anything about God, all we have to do is to look at Christ.

Who being the brightness of his glory, and the express image of his person...

Hebrews 1:3

The best teacher of loyalty is Jesus Christ Himself. He was loyal to his father and to his father's vision. He never deviated from his line of duty. He was loyal even when it cost Him his life on the cross. Christ is the person you must emulate. Why do people call us Christians? Because we are supposed to be Christ-like.

As you read this chapter, decide to emulate these characteristics of Christ-like loyalty. Be the person that is described in the next few pages. Be a devoted and loyal person.

Eleven Christ-Like Characteristics

■   **A Person Who Openly Acknowledges His Father**

Therefore the Jews sought to kill him, because he not only broken the sabbath, but SAID ALSO THAT GOD WAS HIS FATHER, making himself equal with God.

John 5:18

Some people do not want anyone to know about their origins. If you follow me closely, you will know where I came from and how I was trained in the ministry. I am not self-made. I have been influenced greatly by many people.

A loyal person openly speaks of his father. He is not ashamed to say whom he has followed. He is not ashamed to say whose messages have inspired him. Jesus openly spoke about His father. He always explained that he had been sent. His proof that He had been sent lay in the fact that He did the same things that His father did. **A loyal person takes pride in the fact that he has a superior.**

...the same works that I do, bear witness of me, THAT THE FATHER HATH SENT ME.

John 5:36

He spoke so much about his father that it annoyed some people.

Therefore the Jews sought the more to kill him...

John 5:18

I have noticed that certain ministers refuse to speak of their relationship with their seniors. Watch such people because they are not manifesting Christ-like qualities. It is Lucifer who forgot that he was created and appointed. If you have to be reminded about your origins you have a problem.

Thou art the anointed cherub that covereth; and I HAVE SET THEE SO...

Ezekiel 28:14

Someone who does not acknowledge openly and freely where he is from is usually not a grateful person. Such a person usually has a hidden agenda. Perhaps he is after greatness for himself.

■   **A Person Who Follows His Superior's Example at Work**

A loyal subordinate will continue working as long as his superior is working. I have many loyal assistants. Hardly would they go home if I were still around working. Jesus said, "My father is working and because of that I am going to stay around and work."

But Jesus answered them, MY FATHER WORKETH hitherto, AND I WORK.

John 5:17

Dear assistant, how can you sleep when your father is working? A good leader is often the last one to leave. As they say, "The captain is the last one to leave the ship." A good assistant stays with his captain until the end.

Watch out for those who have no time or energy for extra work. Watch out for those who see the leader's hard working attitude as a vexation that makes everyone weary! How can you think that your father is doing unnecessary things? Jesus said, "My father is working and therefore, I must work." Do not think that you are being over-worked. Have the attitude of Jesus.

■   **A Person Who Does Only What He Sees His Leader Doing**

Then answered Jesus and said unto them, Verily verily I say unto you, the son can do nothing of himself BUT WHAT HE SEETH THE FATHER DO...

John 5:19

When you are assisting your father, there are many things you can do. You can do what you think is right or you can do what you see your father do. Let us choose to learn from Jesus. He only did what he saw his father doing. He was loyal to His father and to His father's ideals. He preached what His father would have preached and He did what His father would have done.

Jesus, Why Don't You Heal Everyone?

One day, Jesus did something mysterious. He went into a hospital where there was a multitude of sick people, yet he healed only one person and left the others to their fate.

95

... And Jesus went up to Jerusalem. Now there is a Jerusalem by the sheep market a pool, which is called in the Hebrew tongue Bethesda, having five porches. In these lay A GREAT MULTITUDE OF IMPOTENT FOLK, of blind, halt, withered, waiting for the moving of the water. ...And a certain man was there, which had an infirmity thirty and eight years... Jesus saith unto him, rise take up thy bed, and walk... And he that was healed wist not who it was: for JESUS HAD CONVEYED HIMSELF AWAY, a multitude being in that place.

John 5:1-3, 5,8,13

Later when He was questioned about what He had done, He explained; "I only do what my father does." Jesus saw His father healing only one person and that is what He did. He ministered to only one person! After ministering to one person, He conveyed Himself away. He didn't bother to pray for anyone else. It probably wouldn't have worked anyway!

No Power!

One day at a programme, I decided to pray for everyone present. As I prayed for the people, I felt the power of God was absent. I prayed quietly to myself and said, "Oh Lord, where are you?" Then the Holy Spirit spoke to my spirit and said, "Who asked you to pray for everyone?" Suddenly, I knew I was doing the wrong thing. I was on my own trying to pray for everyone. God wanted me to pray for some people and not for everyone.

You see, with our natural mind, we would do things in a particular way. But Jesus wanted to do only what his father was doing. With my natural mind, I expected that Jesus would heal every single sick person he came into contact with. I expected that he would empty hospitals and heal everyone. But that is not what He did in John chapter five.

Every servant can choose to do his own thing. Are you a loyal minister of Christ? Are you doing what you want to do or are you doing what he is doing? There are many nice things that you can be involved in, but are they the will of God?

Perhaps everybody is opening a school, but is that what the Lord is doing? Perhaps everyone is travelling around ministering, is that what the Lord is doing?

Years ago I had several opportunities to minister in different churches in the world. At that time, the Lord was leading me to stay within the Lighthouse network. I did what I saw my father doing. This has resulted in several large Lighthouse churches all over the world. Is everyone breaking away and becoming a rebel? Do not follow the crowd. Do what you see your father doing. Is your father a rebel? Is your father breaking away?

If you want to succeed in ministry, learn to do exactly what your leader is doing. **You will grow faster when you emulate your leader exactly.** Do you want to progress faster in ministry? Life is too short for you not to learn from your fathers. Jesus did exactly what he had seen his father do and he was a successful minister. Many of my pastors preach what I preach and teach what I teach. They run the programs in their churches in the way they see me do it.

Don't Be a Hero!

I have noticed something! My "children" in the Lord, who follow me closely and do what they see me do, make greater strides in ministry. Those who experiment and play around with unproven methods often take much longer to advance in ministry. I want to say it again! Don't be a hero! Your life is too short for you to play around with it. Your life is too short to use part of it to discover things that have already been discovered.

It is time for you to move quickly in ministry. The fields are white unto harvest. Do what you see your father in ministry do. Follow him closely. Avoid his mistakes and learn all you can from him. A loyal person takes pride in the fact that he is able to do exactly what his father does.

...THE SAME WORKS THAT I DO, BEAR WITNESS OF ME, that the father hath sent me.

John 5:36

The loyalty of Christ to his father's methods paid off. Jesus was the ultimate minister. Learn his secrets and you will be great in the ministry.

■　**A Person Who Does Not Seek His Own Will, but the Will of His Leader**

I can of mine own self do nothing: as I hear, I judge: and my judgment is just; because I SEEK NOT MINE OWN WILL, BUT THE WILL OF THE FATHER which hath sent me.

John 5:30

What a blessing it is to have an assistant who is not seeking his own will. I once had a pastor who joined my team with his own vision. He was not seeking to accomplish my vision. His aim was to accomplish his dream. Jesus said very clearly, "I seek not my own will, but the will of Him who sent me."

Let me ask you today, "Who sent you? Whose vision are you following?" When there are two or more visions within one team, you have a division. When there is division there is a lot of pain and hurt. Even if your small toe were to separate from your body you would experience a lot of pain and you would not be able to sleep.

I had a pastor who decided to use me as a stepping-stone to his ministry. I had no idea that this young man was using me to accomplish his vision. I thought he was helping me to accomplish my vision. He used me to gain visibility and was introduced as a minister. His secret plan was to leave us after some years. Indeed, some years after he joined, he pushed through with his vision and separated himself in a very painful move. We were taken aback! But this is what happens when there are assistants with their own hidden agenda and programs.

Develop the loyalty of Christ. He said very clearly, "I seek not my own will, but the will of my father which hath sent me." If you have been sent to begin a church in another country or locality, decide to accomplish the will of those who sent you.

■ A Person Who Does Not Bear Witness of Himself

IF I BEAR WITNESS OF MYSELF, MY WITNESS IS NOT TRUE. There is another that beareth witness of me; and I know that the witness which he witnesseth of me is true.

John 5:31, 32

When you bear witness of yourself, you promote and exalt yourself. Jesus did none of these. He exalted His father and spoke constantly of where He derived His authority. That is the loyalty of Christ. A person who exalts and promotes himself is not sent from God. Are you a loyal person? There is no need to elevate yourself beyond your current position. The Lord who sent you will do that for you.

There are pastors whose best sermons are about themselves and what they have achieved. If you are a prophet, there is no need to exalt yourself. God has a way of exalting people He has called.

How can ye believe, which receive honour one of another, and seek not the honour that cometh from God only?

John 5:44

There is no need to be a pushy or forward minister. There is no need to invite yourself everywhere, claiming you want to be a blessing to others. Allow God to lift you up Himself.

■ A Person Who Does Not Allow the Words of Men to Influence Him

But I receive not testimony from man...

John 5:34

A leader must be very careful about what men say to him. Human beings are fickle and can misdirect you. They will tell you that you are an apostle, prophet or evangelist. They will say to you, "Do not submit yourself to any man. You can do it yourself." Others will say to you, "You can also write books. He is not the only one who is anointed." Assistants, watch out! They will tell you, "I prefer it when you preach. I wish you were given more opportunities to minister."

You Can Break Away!

A senior minister once told my associate, "Do not see yourself as an assistant. You are a great man of God. God has called you to do great things." He continued, "Can you not see that anytime there is trouble in the church, you are the one who is sent to put out the fires?" "You can move out on your own and you will be great in ministry". My associate was taken aback because this advice was coming from a senior minister. Moreover, this 'advisor' happened to be a friend of mine. My pastor was not taken in by this treacherous suggestion. My associate told me later, "I decided never to interact with this minister again." He had concluded to himself: "This is a very dangerous person."

Many people listen to this kind of advice and embark on a wild goose chase. Understand that your credentials do not come by what men say about you. Men can easily misdirect you in the ministry.

I RECEIVE NOT HONOUR FROM MEN. But I know you, that ye have not the love of God in you.
John 5:41, 42

Jesus was careful not to receive direction from human beings. He took inspiration directly from the Father. **When people criticize you, remember that it is what God says that matters.**

Years ago when some people called me "Jim Jones", I could not believe my ears. They derided and denigrated me. To denigrate means: to blacken the reputation of someone. I have been blackened many times! I have been blackened by friends! I have been blackened by pastors! I have been blackened by neighbours! However, I am still around! This is because my promotion does not and will not come from these people. It comes from the Lord!

The promotion I have received in the ministry is not from men. Some men have mostly said negative things about me. It must be painful for these same men to watch as the Lord slowly but surely lifts me up.

> ...Thou preparest a table before me in the presence of mine enemies...
>
> **Psalm 23:5**

The loyalty of Christ will pay off in the end.

■   **A Loyal Person Does Not Seek to Impress People**

> **How can ye believe, WHICH RECEIVE HONOUR ONE OF ANOTHER, and seek not the honour that cometh from God only?**
>
> **John 5:44**

A loyal person does not try to impress others. One dangerous trait for leaders to have is a desire to impress people. Paul said that he had overcome the need to impress or please anybody.

> **For do I now persuade men, or God? or do I seek to please men? for if I yet pleased men, I should not be the servant of Christ.**
>
> **Galatians 1:10**

Why is this character trait a dangerous thing? Because you cannot please everyone, you will end up hurting some and pleasing the others.

Ministers who cannot take hard decisions because they want to make everybody happy, end up destroying their own churches.

Years ago I had an assistant who was a very nice person. I liked him very much and so did many others. I still like him because he is a nice person. He was nice to be with and he chatted freely with all the members of the church. The members gravitated to him naturally although he was my assistant.

Soon, external ministers who were not part of our church knew him. With the process of time, some of these external ministers began to be inimical towards my ministry. This pleasant brother tried to balance his loyalties between myself and the external ministers. Mind you, he never showed any outward signs of ill will. He was a nice person through and through. However, you cannot please everyone! There comes a time when you must stand up for your conviction. A time came when I realised that his heart was not with me. He could not please those other ministers and me. A time came when we had to go our separate ways.

You are not safe with a leader who tries to impress everyone.

■ **A Loyal Person Seeks Only the Approval of His Leader**

There is another that BEARETH WITNESS OF ME; and I know that the witness which he witnesseth of me is true.

John 5:32

A loyal person knows that it is what his father says that really matters. Men may disapprove of you, but with God's approval, you are going places. Every minister must realize that it is God who opens certain doors and closes others. Seek the approval of the one who really matters.

Human beings may rant and rave about you. They may say all sorts of evil things, but if you have the approval of your father, man, you are covered.

■ **A Loyal Person Constantly Hears the Voice of His Master**

...YE HAVE NEITHER HEARD HIS VOICE at any time, nor seen his shape. And ye have not his word abiding in you...

John 5:37, 38

Jesus heard the voice of His father; He was constantly in touch with His father. Loyalty is greatly helped by communication. A person often becomes disloyal when he stays out of touch for a long time.

I encourage my pastors to stay in touch all the time. Those who listen to tapes and hear the voice of their leader are more prone to be faithful. Those who read the books, listen to the tapes and watch the videos are in constant fellowship with their father.

Distance, separation and a lack of communication have a way of breaking up friendships. That is why most denominations have yearly meetings and gatherings of all sorts. If you want to encourage loyalty within a system you are creating, increase the number of gatherings that you have.

■ **A Loyal Person Loves His Leader and Loves the Lord**

But I know you, that YE HAVE NOT THE LOVE OF GOD in you.

John 5:42

Love never fails. When there is genuine love within an association, church or group, there is a bond which is difficult to break. Things are kept together by bonds and linkages. Do you want a bond that is stronger than super glue? Try love! Love is as strong as death. It is a bond that cannot be easily broken.

... Put on charity (love), which is the BOND OF PERFECTNESS.

Colossians 3:14

Let me ask you a question, "Do you love your head?" If you do, then it is likely that you will be faithful to him. I would prefer to work with people who love me rather than those who are with me because of what they can get from me. That is why I prefer to have an office which is more of a family than a business.

A Loyal Person Flows with Loyal People

For HAD YE BELIEVED MOSES, YE WOULD HAVE BELIEVED ME: for he wrote of me.

John 5:46

Christ 'flowed' with Moses. He spoke about Moses. He read Moses' books. Note that Moses was one of God's faithful servants. Jesus told the crowds that they did not believe in Moses or his teachings. A loyal person associates with loyal people. A loyal person believes in the teachings of other faithful people. His friends are good people. As they say, "Birds of a feather flock together."

Jesus' ministry was in line with the teaching of Moses, one of God's most faithful and loyal servants. Who are your friends? Whose teachings do you flow with? Are you always siding with rebels and wrongdoers? If you want to know if someone is loyal, take a good look at his friends.

Chapter 9

The Loyalty of the Father

This chapter could also be entitled, *How to Be a Loyal Senior Pastor* or *How to Be a Loyal Chief Executive*. You must realize that Jesus was sent to the Earth as an emissary of the Father. His duty was to present the views of our heavenly Father to this world. He was supposed to let everyone know what the Father was like.

Many people do not know what God is like. By knowing Jesus they get to know what the Creator of Heaven and Earth is really like. Jesus could have misrepresented the Father, but He did not. The Father (who represents the sending organization) could have failed Jesus when He was on this earth. But Almighty God was loyal to the one He had sent.

Many senior pastors are not loyal to their followers. As I have observed the behaviour of certain senior leaders, bishops, managing directors, etc.; I have often said to myself, "I could never work in such an environment." Some senior pastors are so inconsistent and unconcerned about the welfare and future of their subordinates that it would be unwise to follow such people.

If you want to have a stable following, you must decide to develop a pattern of loyalty towards those who support you.

In this chapter, I want us to see how our heavenly Father demonstrated his loyalty to Jesus Christ whom He had sent into this world. The loyalty of the Father demonstrates the type of person every manager or senior pastor needs to be.

Six Characteristics of a Loyal Senior Minister

1. **A leader who works**

   But Jesus answered them, MY FATHER WORKETH HITHERTO, AND I WORK.

   John 5:17

There are some leaders who do not work; they just give orders and go to sleep. Jesus was under the authority of His Father and he spoke of His Father and said, "My Father works and I also work."

Do not just enjoy the *privileges* of leaders. People love to work when they see their leader working. The sight of their leader working gives them much inspiration. Do you want to motivate your workers and followers? Let them know that you work even harder than they do!

2.   A leader who is seen

Then answered Jesus and said unto them, Verily, verily, I say unto you, The Son can do nothing of himself, but WHAT HE SEETH THE FATHER DO: for what things soever he doeth, these also doeth the Son likewise.

John 5:19

Everybody wants to follow someone they can see. There is a style of leadership in which the boss is more of a Prime Minister than anything else. If the senior pastor is more of a Prime Minister than a pastor, he is seen very occasionally. He comes in with high security and does not talk to the common man. He is whisked in and whisked out! But our heavenly Father is not somebody that Jesus could not see. Jesus could see all that his Father was doing and follow Him easily.

When David came on the scene, he won the hearts of the Israelites. He was a young man and a good warrior. But he won the hearts of the Israelites because he was more visible than Saul. The people could see their leader and they were happy with him.

But all Israel and Judah loved David, because he went out and came in before them.

1 Samuel 18:16

People are more loyal to people they see than to people they cannot see. That is why members of churches tend to be more loyal to their resident pastor whom they see every day, than to the general overseer whom they rarely see.

3. A leader who loves his subordinates

For the Father LOVETH the son...

John 5:20a

The Father loved the one He had sent. Be a leader who loves his followers. Many leaders do not care about the people they lead. **When the people you lead are sure that you love them, they will be willing to do almost anything for you.** Loyalty is deeper than what you see on the outside. It goes beyond giving orders that are obeyed! Loyalty is of the heart. When you can win the hearts of the people and convince them that you care for them, they will be loyal to you. This is exactly what Absalom did.

Absalom, although an evil person, used a principle that works for everyone. He used the principle of showing love to the people in order to gain their loyalties. Love is a seed. If you sow it, you will reap it!

I want you to notice how Absalom won the hearts and loyalties of the people of Israel.

And Absalom rose up early, and stood beside the way of the gate: and it was so, that when any man that had a controversy came to the king for judgment, then Absalom called unto him, and said, Of what city art thou? And he said, Thy servant is of one of the tribes of Israel. And Absalom said unto him, See, thy matters are good and right; but there is no man deputed of the king to hear thee. Absalom said moreover, Oh that I were made judge in the land, that every man which hath any suit or cause might come unto me, and I would do him justice!

2 Samuel 15:2-4

Absalom asked people about their problems. If you are a good leader, you will be interested in people's personal problems. It helps to win their hearts. People turn their loyalties towards a leader who shows genuine care and concern for their well-being.

When Jesus said, "the Father loveth the Son", He was giving us a great revelation about how to treat those who work for us.

Absalom came from the outside and won the hearts of the people from David, the king. Absalom showed that he wanted to help the people.

...Oh that I were made judge in the land...
2 Samuel 15:4

Absalom said he wanted a chance to be judge. His message was simple; "Oh, if only I had a chance to help." Gradually, the hearts of the people were drawn to Absalom. **If you are the senior pastor of the church, you must draw the hearts of the people to yourself so that they will be loyal to you.** Show them that you care. Show them that you are interested.

You must not allow their hearts to be 'stolen' by any one. You must do this if you want to keep your church in one piece. Do not allow a rebellious assistant to sit at the gate of your church or company. **Do not allow a rebellious worker to have access to the sheep that God has given you.** If their hearts are with the assistant, you have a dangerous situation on your hands. One day, when the assistant decides to leave, he will move away with a large section of your people.

And on this manner did Absalom unto all Israel that came to the king for judgment: so ABSALOM STOLE THE HEARTS of the men of Israel.
2 Samuel 15:6

4.   A leader who is open to his subordinates

For the Father loveth the son, and sheweth him all things that himself doeth...
John 5:20

When Jesus was on earth, He knew that He could trust His heavenly Father absolutely. This was because His Father had shown Him all that He was doing. I have discovered that openness breeds loyalty. I have always endeavoured to be open to those I lead so that they can trust me. Some ministers are mysteriously prosperous. When you ask them, "How did you come by this house or car?" They will answer; "It is the blessing of the Lord." They will continue, "God has made a way where there was no way."

We thank God for His blessings and for giving you more than you carry. But in practical terms, how did you come by the things you have? What is the channel or vessel that God used to promote you? When people know the source of your blessings they are more relaxed in your presence. When they feel that you are not cheating anyone, they tend to be more loyal.

That is why the Father showed the Lord Jesus everything He was doing. Jesus knew what His future was. Jesus knew that His present suffering was for a season. He knew that He had a good Father who had His best interests at heart. He was prepared to do anything and to go anywhere to please His Father.

Wouldn't you like to have subordinates with that sort of attitude? How many workers would be prepared to die for their bosses? Yet, Jesus died on the cross because His 'boss' wanted Him to! Jesus described His death on the cross as the cup that his 'boss' had given Him to drink. He described His sacrifice as a drink. How many employees describe their hard work as a drink?

Then said Jesus unto Peter... THE CUP WHICH MY FATHER HATH GIVEN ME, SHALL I NOT DRINK IT?

John 18:11

Many ordinary people have very little confidence in the leadership of their countries. We all know that many things are hidden. We know that millions of dollars are probably being stashed away by the leaders of their countries.

Openness Generates Trust!

Corruption is often exposed after the leaders were removed. Recently, when a Head of State in Africa died, a billion dollars of petty cash was discovered in his home. I was personally taken aback! Confidence in the leadership is very low when everything is shrouded in secret. We realize that we will only know everything after the removal of dictators. The salaries and benefits of the American president for the rest of his life are public knowledge. Why is this? To generate confidence in the government.

Mistrust Leads to Separation

When people feel that they are not trusted, they begin to separate themselves. They feel hurt and rejected. "Why should I stay around if I'm not trusted?" They say to themselves.

A good leader must not do things that make his followers or subordinates feel like they are not trusted. It is a sure seed that can lead to disloyalty. Those who are not involved in sensitive areas, such as money, should not feel that they are being excluded because of mistrust. They must be made to understand that everyone has a schedule and it happens that their schedule does not involve financial things!

For the Father loveth him and showeth him all things!

5. A leader who gives public commendation of his followers

And the Father himself which hath sent me, HATH BORNE WITNESS OF ME...

John 5:37

A good manager is someone who gives public approval of his workers. **Praise people in public and correct them in private.** A good leader knows that praising his subordinates is not going to weaken his position. It is a good thing to show public approval for your subordinates. It breeds a spirit of confidence and loyalty. Jesus often said that His Father had testified of Him in public. The Father did many public things that demonstrated his approval of Jesus.

Many bishops, head pastors and general overseers do not want to publicly approve of their juniors. It just does not occur to some people to recommend their workers. Some feel that it is unnecessary. Others are insecure and so do not do it. I often wonder why some people who like to be praised and encouraged refuse to praise and encourage others.

One day, Jesus raised Lazarus from the dead. The prayer that the Lord Jesus prayed at the cemetery was very revealing. *He did not pray for anointing or power to raise the dead.* He had to explain to his Father why He was even praying at the tomb site. He told His father, "I know that you always hear my prayers. It is because of the people around that I am praying. I want them to know how you approve of me."

Then they took away the stone from the place where the dead was laid. And Jesus lifted up his eyes, and said, Father, I thank thee that thou hast heard me. And I knew that thou hearest me always: but because of the people which stand by I said it, THAT THEY MAY BELIEVE THAT THOU HAS SENT ME.

John 11:41, 42

A leader who constantly disgraces his subordinates in public will not have many loyal followers. No one is perfect! I have corrected many of my subordinates in ministry. But I always do it in private. You would never know about the discussions that have gone on behind closed doors. It does not concern you anyway. How can a leader have confidence if he is constantly rebuked in front of those he leads?

6. **A leader who trusts the judgment and decisions of his subordinates**

For the Father judgeth no man, but HATH COMMITTED ALL JUDGMENT UNTO THE SON:

John 5:22

The Father, once again exemplifies great leadership as He demonstrates trust in His messenger. Jesus was sent to this earth as a messenger of the Father. Jesus was given a lot of responsibility. He was trusted with decisions. He was trusted with the judgment of this Earth. He had a large amount of independence committed to Him. This is a mystery, because in another breath Jesus said, "I can of my own self do nothing: as I hear, I judge." (John 5:30) Even though Jesus had been given a large amount of latitude in which to operate, He had decided to depend on the decisions and judgments His Father would make.

A good leader can generate loyalty in people by giving them a freehand in many of the decisions that affect their own lives. The Lord showed this to me many years ago and I have implemented it with great success. **I know that people become more loyal when they are involved in the decision-making process.** It gives them power, freedom and independence. These are things that every human being needs!

Long ago, I decentralised the decisions about salaries and benefits for the few employees we have. Almost everybody who is employed in my set-up is involved in determining his or her own conditions of service. I prefer to invite people to the "soup pot" and ask them to dish themselves. If they take out all the meat, there will be none left for all of us and we will all starve.

I often tell the different boards who take these decisions, "Just make sure you don't kill the chicken which lays the eggs." I remind them, "If you kill the chicken which lays our eggs, we will all starve in the future."

Once people have a mature mind as they approach the "soup pot", they take sound and rational decisions. Most of the time, I don't even know what people are paid in their different regions. For all you know, they may earn more than I do. I trust them to be sensible. Of course, there are supervisory checks and balances in place. But people know that they have been trusted with the judgment. When people realize that they have been entrusted with high responsibility, they often mature overnight.

Jesus said that the Father had committed all judgment to the Son. Allow people to use their brains. Do not assume that you are the only wise person who can take decisions. After all, as someone said, "You are not always right!" Do not be afraid to trust people. **Sow a seed of trust and you will reap more trust.** Learn from your heavenly Father today. Be a follower of Almighty God.

Be ye therefore followers of God, as dear children.

Ephesians 5:1

Chapter 10

The Three Tests of Loyalty

But he knoweth the way that I take: when he hath tried me, I SHALL COME FORTH AS GOLD.

Job 23:10

There are many yellow metals in the world. Which one of them is real gold? I once asked a jeweller in Malaysia; "How would I know whether my wedding ring is made out of real gold or not?" I will never forget what he said, "There are many tests, but the main test is to pass it through fire." He told me, "All other metals will change colour when subjected to fire."

He continued, "Gold is the only metal which will come out shining brighter. It will not change colour in any way."

You can never tell the false from the real until you subject it to a test.

Many things will test the loyalty and faithfulness of a Christian. When I decided to pursue the ministry instead of medicine, my commitment was tested many times. My commitment to the church has been tested on several occasions. There are three main things that will test everyone's loyalty: *distance, time* and *fire*. If you pass these tests, then your loyalty is real.

1. The Test of Distance

But it is good to be zealously affected always in a good thing, AND NOT ONLY WHEN I AM PRESENT WITH YOU.

Galatians 4:18

Paul had to exhort a branch of his church in Galatia to remain faithful even though he was not physically present with them. Many people are not loyal when they are away from the leader.

Many companies do not work efficiently unless the manager is physically present. Because of this, many businesses cannot expand.

Can the Boss Be Everywhere?

If you are working under someone, your loyalty will be tested by distance. As they say, "out of sight, out of mind". It is important for you to be faithful even when your leader is away from you. People who have passed this test are the ones who are truly faithful. **The only way for a large network to continue expanding is for people to be faithful whether the leader is present or not.**

In some churches, the pastor just has to turn his head and a sarcastic comment will be made. You must not only say nice things when a person is present with you. You must say nice things about him even when he is away. It is good to be zealously affected always in a good thing and especially when your leader is not present with you. I can tell whether people are loyal to me or not by what they say about me when I am not present.

It is good to be zealously affected always in a good thing, AND NOT ONLY WHEN I AM PRESENT WITH YOU.

Galatians 4:18

My Loyal Friend

I remember someone who claimed to be my friend. When I was with him, he would say nice things like, "I am committed to you. I have a relationship with you." He also said things like, "I know you are loyal to me. You and I have a good relationship." However, when I was not with this person he would say terrible things about me. Some of the things were so shocking that it was hard for me to believe!

One day someone said to me, "If you ever heard what this man said about you behind your back, you would not go near him any more!" What this person was telling me was not strange.

You see, I had heard of alarming statements made by this man about me. I had received so many reports of the cruel discussions he had had about me. This "loyal" friend was not loyal after all! When he was with me, he said nice things. As soon as we parted company, he stabbed me in the back and 'weeded out' my legs! A little distance and the ugly head of disloyalty reared itself. He failed the 'distance test' of loyalty repeatedly.

Loyalty is not what you say or do when a person is with you. It is what you do and say when you are apart.

It is good to be zealously affected always in a good thing, AND NOT ONLY WHEN I AM PRESENT WITH YOU.

Galatians 4:18

2. The Test of Time

Very few people can imagine the ability of time to test our resolve to stay loyal to our words.

I marvel that ye are SO SOON REMOVED from him that called you into the grace of Christ unto another gospel:

Galatians 1:6

The Apostle Paul was shocked that a group of Christians could so quickly change their minds and commitment.

Early and Late Disloyalty

In some cases people become disloyal very early in the course of events. This is what I call *early disloyalty*. People suffering from *early disloyalty* are not able to withstand the test of time. In other cases, people become disloyal after much more time has elapsed – this is late disloyalty. Individuals who experience *'late disloyalty'* have a greater ability to withstand the tests of time, but eventually fall away.

And he said, therefore said I unto you, that no man can come unto me, except it were given unto him of my Father. FROM THAT TIME MANY OF HIS DISCIPLES WENT BACK, and walked no more with him. Then said Jesus unto the twelve, Will ye also go away?

Then Simon Peter answered him, LORD, TO WHOM SHALL WE GO? thou hast the words of eternal life. And we believe and are sure that thou art Christ, the Son of the living God. Jesus answered them, Have not I chosen you twelve and one of you is a devil?

He spake of JUDAS ISCARIOT the son of Simon: for he it was that should betray him, BEING ONE OF THE TWELVE.

John 6:65-71

You will notice from this passage that after a short while in the ministry, several of the disciples deserted camp. They left the church and refused to be part of Jesus' ministry anymore. *From that time many of his disciples went back, and walked no more with him (John 6:66).* This is a good example of 'early disloyalty'. These disciples failed the test of time very quickly indeed.

However, the twelve apostles were not so quick to fall away. Even Judas Iscariot was not moved. But Jesus knew that with the passage of *more time,* Judas would betray him. That is why he said, "Have I not chosen you twelve and one of you is a devil? He knew it was just a matter of time before there would be some more manifestations of disloyalty.

Can you stand the test of time? Will you be there when everyone is gone? How much longer will you last in the ministry? For how much longer will you preach the things God told you to preach? How much more time has to elapse before you rebel against your leader? Are you going to be an early leaver, a late leaver or will you stay until the end?

Decide to be a survivor! Develop staying power! Be faithful to the very end! Be loyal to God until your very last breath! Be loyal to your pastor and to your church until the end. You will definitely receive your reward from God. I recommend that you read my book on 'Backsliding'. It will help you to develop your staying power.

3. The Test of Fire

Fire represents all kinds of pressures that will be brought to bear against you. These pressures could be in the form of a financial test. When you work in an organisation, a transfer or an instruction you do not like could be another test. Fire could be spiritual, social, marital or financial! I want to challenge every leader not to be afraid of the fires that God will allow you to go through. It is those who come out of the fire unscathed who are most valuable to God.

Marital difficulties, financial difficulties, hurts and offences should not make you disloyal to your God. Fire purges unwanted elements from our lives. God refines us through these experiences.

And he shall sit as a refiner and purifier of silver: and he shall purify the sons of Levi, and purge them as gold and silver, that they may offer unto the Lord an offering in righteousness.

Malachi 3:3

God often puts the heat on his servants in order to bring the best out of them. When you have passed through the tests, you will shine and you will become more attractive. Do you want more people to be attracted to your ministry? Then pass the tests of fire that come your way!

My brethren, count it all joy when ye fall into divers temptations; Knowing this, that the trying of your faith worketh patience.

James 1:2, 3

On many occasions, I have been subjected to various tests. I have been subjected to tests from disloyal friends and pastors.

I have suffered mistreatment from authorities in high places. I have been through many journeys for the Lord. I have had several near death experiences in cars and planes. I have experienced deep hurts from various unexpected sources.

I am not the only one who has been tested in the ministry. God allows all Christians to be offended. He will then observe whether you will obey his Word or not. Will you forgive the one who has offended you? When you walk in forgiveness, you attract God's mercy. Blessed are the merciful because they shall receive God's mercy. **If you fail the test of hurts and offences, you exclude yourself from the mercy of God.**

When bitterness is in your spirit, you will no longer receive from God and he no longer answers your prayers.

Many years ago, a minister said something which I took seriously. He said, *"It is important to always maintain a sweet spirit!"* We must learn to live without bitterness.

When you go through the fire of financial difficulties, please do not succumb to the pressure. Do not become a murmurer. Do not become a complainer and do not become a thief!

When you come under pressure in your marriage, please do not give up. Do not separate or divorce. Fight to achieve happiness. The world is full of people with failed marriages. Everyone is looking for someone who has been able to stay faithful in spite of the tests. The tests of marriage come to everyone. To survive, you need determination and a whole lot of faith. Be a survivor! I see you making it!

What Have You Survived?

Someone asked me: "What have you been through? What have you survived?" "What have you suffered?" You see, the things a person has survived speak volumes about him. The credentials of survived tests are greater than the credentials of any educational institution.

When Paul wanted to show who he really was, he told the people what he had been through! He told them what he had survived. He showed them what he had suffered. The tests you pass tell a story about who you really are. Notice how Paul used a long list of experiences he had survived to show that he was a legitimate minister.

ARE THEY MINISTERS OF CHRIST? (I speak as a fool) I AM MORE; in labours more abundant, in stripes above measure, in PRISONS more frequent, in DEATHS oft. Of the Jews five times received I forty STRIPES save one.

Thrice was I BEATEN with rods, once was I stoned, thrice I suffered SHIPWRECK, a night and a day I have been in the deep; In JOURNEYINGS often, in perils of waters, in perils of ROBBERS, in perils by mine own countrymen, in perils by the heathen, in perils in the city, in perils in the wilderness, in perils in the sea, in perils among false brethren;

In WEARINESS and PAINFULNESS, in WATCHINGS often, in hunger and thirst, in FASTINGS often, in cold and NAKEDNESS. Beside those things that are without, that which cometh upon me daily, the care of all the churches. Who is weak, and I am not weak? Who is offended and I burn not?

2 Corinthians 11:23-29

Chapter 11

The Rewards of Loyalty

What Is the Reward of Disloyalty?

It is a known fact that the rebels of the Bible did not end up well. A curse is a solemn invocation of divine wrath on a person, which results in evil or harm. Look closely at the rebels of the Bible and decide for yourself whether a disloyal person is blessed or cursed.

Execution

The end of all rebels is one and the same – execution. Rebellion is an essentially evil thing. The Bible teaches us that rebellion is as witchcraft.

For rebellion is as the sin of witchcraft...

1 Samuel 15:23

The Biblical punishment for witchcraft is execution.

Thou shalt not suffer a witch to live.

Exodus 22:18

God does not support rebellion in any form or fashion. Do not involve yourself in any kind of rebellion. The people who get involved in revolts are often simpleminded. Many of them do not know what is afoot.

And with Absalom went two hundred men out of Jerusalem, that were called; and THEY WENT IN THEIR SIMPLICITY, AND THEY KNEW NOT ANY THING.

2 Samuel 15:11

Many people run into rebellion because of their innocence and ignorance. If Absalom's followers had known exactly what they were doing, I believe they would not have followed him.

The fruit of rebellion throughout the Bible is very clear – execution. God will divinely displace and replace you with someone else. Your seat will be taken by another who is worthier than you. You will be banished into obscurity and oblivion. There will be a curse on you and your family. Just study the following list of executions:

Six Famous Executions

Lucifer

And the great dragon was cast out, that old serpent, called the Devil, and Satan, which deceiveth the whole world: he was cast out into the earth, and his angels were cast out with him.

Revelation 12:9

Absalom

And ten young men... compassed about and smote Absalom, and slew him.

2 Samuel 18:15

Ahithophel

...Ahithophel... hanged himself, and died...

2 Samuel 17:23

Shemei

So the king commanded Benaiah... which went out, and fell upon him [Shemei], that he died...

1 Kings 2:46

Adonijah

And king Solomon sent by the hand of Benaiah the son of Jehoiada; and he fell upon him (Adonijah) that he died.

1 Kings 2:25

Judas

And he (Judas)... went and hanged himself.
                                        Matthew 27:5

Is Loyalty Rewarded?

...Well done, thou good and faithful servant: thou hast been faithful over a few things. I will make thee ruler over many things: enter thou into the joy of thy Lord.
                                        Matthew 25:21

This Scripture outlines two important blessings that follow loyal or faithful people.

• Loyalty Is Rewarded with Growth

Loyal people receive an increase (many things) from the Lord. As you pray for growth in your church and ministry, remember that loyalty is the master key to expansion. Loyalty makes you persist in the same thing until it bears fruit.

I suggest that you engage in a little research. You will discover that large growing churches differ in style, strategy and emphasis. Some of them are soul-winning churches and others have an emphasis on miracles and the Holy Spirit. Some megachurches are oriented towards social services and political issues. Yet still, some large churches have an emphasis on prosperity and dominion! All of these churches differ greatly in many areas. However, a closer look will reveal that there are some common denominators in every large church.

Almost all large churches are led by pastors who have remained faithful to the same church for a long time. When pastors move around every few years, they do not experience consistent growth. If you are a minister who desires expansion and growth, you must be prepared to stay in one place for a long time. Ask God for the privilege of investing your entire life in one location.

I am in the ministry for the rest of my life. My commitment to the people around me is a lifetime commitment and vice versa. I am loyal to them and I pray that they will be loyal to me. The blessing of largeness is reserved for faithful and loyal people.

• Loyal People Experience the Favour of God

The second blessing of faithfulness is entering the joy of the Lord. This means experiencing the favour of God. When the favour of God is upon you, your enemies will not flourish around you.

By this I know that thou favourest me, because mine enemy doth not triumph over me.

Psalm 41:11

Be a loyal person so that you can have great growth in your business or ministry. Be a loyal person so that you can have God's favour over all that you set your hand to do.

Chapter 12

Seven Methods for Dealing with Disloyalty

Every manager, businessperson and pastor must learn seven important methods to deal with all forms of disloyalty.

1. The Teaching Method

This method involves teaching the Word of God regularly. This method is a preventive process that every wise minister or leader should adopt. There are two ways to manage an organisation: crisis management or *preventive* management.

In crisis management, you move from one crisis to another, solving the issues as they come up. In *preventive* management you constantly teach and immunize the people against the problem you are trying to avoid.

I would suggest to you that your church or business should adopt the preventive style of management. Those who have a crisis management style are often stressed out and never able to do the things they have to in order to take their business or church forward.

Teaching your people constantly is a sure way of preventing a whole array of problems. This is why I hold Shepherds' (leaders) Camps and Congresses. This is why I constantly have meetings with our pastors and leaders.

The main thing that teaching does is to fight against deception. It is only people who are deceived who go in the way of Absalom or Lucifer. Lucifer was deceived and is the father of deception. Lucifer thought that he could replace God. He said, "I will ascend and be like the Most High." There must be a strong deception for a created being to think of displacing the Almighty God.

The Bible calls the devil "that old serpent who deceives the whole world". If someone can deceive the whole world, then believe me he must be very good at it! That is why the teaching method of dealing with disloyalty is very important.

And the great dragon was cast out, THAT OLD SERPENT, CALLED THE DEVIL, and Satan, which DECEIVETH THE WHOLE WORLD: he was cast out into the earth, and his angels were cast out with him.

Revelation 12:9

Many countries have adopted preventive medicine (primary health care) as the mainstay of their medical programmes. It has become evident that it is easier to prevent diseases than to fight them once they are established.

It is easier to prevent disloyalty by teaching than to clean up after an 'Absalom' has passed through the church. The situation created by a 'Judas' is so messy that you would be better off preventing it.

2. The Nicolaitan Method

But this thou hast, that thou hateth the deeds of the Nicolaitanes, which I also hate.

Revelation 2:6

In this method, the church together with its leadership develops a hatred and aversion for disloyalty and disloyal people. The Nicolaitanes were hated by the Ephesian Church and God recommended them for that!

When people are taught about Judas, Absalom, Ahitophel and so on, they gradually develop a hatred for any form of disloyalty. They are quick to pick it up and reject it.

One brother told a friend in the church, "I want to tell you something in confidence. You know Pastor is really annoying me." He continued, "I know that the series he his preaching is directed against me." He went on, "I am very angry with him."

The brother he was talking to replied, "What is wrong with you? Are you out of your mind? Why are you talking like this? I am going to tell Pastor what you said."

The angry brother was taken aback. .He said, "This loyalty thing has also affected you." Indeed the loyalty "thing" had affected this brother. He immediately reported these unacceptable comments to the pastor. Soon that fire was quenched.

This is the Nicolaitan method – where everyone has a hatred for rebellion and any form of disloyalty.

3. The North Wind Method

The NORTH WIND driveth away rain: so doth an angry countenance a backbiting tongue.

Proverbs 25:23

This scripture teaches us that an angry facial expression can drive away disloyalty. You see, complainers, murmurers and slanderers are looking for someone to talk to. If you give them the chance, they will sit you down and poison you thoroughly. What every leader must realize is that these people must not be given a chance to even speak in our midst.

Some people's words are like cancer. They poison the whole system and have a potential for polluting many people. Would you smile at the sight of a viper in your sitting room? What facial expression would come up if you saw a rattlesnake in your bathtub? Certainly not a smile! I am sure you would have no welcoming facial expressions for the viper. Please do not welcome vipers in the church or in the company.

From today there can be no welcoming smiles for defiant agitators. They must not for one moment feel welcome in our midst! If you cannot smile at a snake do not smile at a disloyal person. Let him know from your facial expression that his presence and his comments are undesirable.

4. The Abrahamic Method

This is the method of peaceful separation. It happens between mature individuals who want to avoid the deadly effects of conflicts.

> **And there was a strife between the herdmen of Abram's cattle and the herdmen of Lot's cattle: and the Canaanite and the Perizzite dwelled then in the land.**
>
> **And Abram said unto Lot, Let there be no strife, I pray thee, between me and thee, and between my herdmen and thy herdmen; for we be brethren. Is not the whole land before thee? SEPARATE THYSELF, I PRAY THEE, FROM ME: if thou wilt take the left hand, then I will go to the right; or if thou depart to the right hand, then I will go to the left.**
>
> **And Lot lifted up his eyes, and beheld all the plain of Jordan, that it was well watered every where, before the Lord destroyed Sodom and Gomorrah, even as the garden of the Lord, like the land of Egypt, as thou comest unto Zoar. Then Lot chose him all the plain of Jordan; and Lot journeyed east: and they separated themselves the one from the other.**
>
> **Genesis 13:7-11**

There was strife between Abraham's men and Lot's men. God gave Abraham wisdom to deal with the situation. He called his nephew Lot and suggested a peaceful separation.

There are some people you should not work with. As long as you labour with them on the same field, there will never be peace. Sometimes people simply do not believe in your calling. They cannot accept that God will use you for anything special.

Do You Believe in My Prayer?

These people must be allowed to separate from you in peace. I once prayed for someone. After the prayer I asked, "Do you believe in my prayer?" The answer was short and simple – "No!" I told this individual to go peacefully to another church. I said, "Over there you will be able to receive."

This is different from a dismissal in which a rebel is thrown out! In this case everyone goes his way and has equal opportunities to do well. With time, the differences will show up. After the separation of Abraham and Lot, there were soon obvious differences between the two parties. These were due to the different relationships that Abraham and Lot had with the Lord. No one can see your spiritual status in the natural. But with time, it becomes clear as to who is really called of God.

And the Lord said unto Abram, after that Lot was separated from him, Lift up now thine eyes, and look from the place where thou art northward, and eastward, and westward: For all the land which thou seest, to thee will I give it, and to thy see for ever.

Genesis 13:14, 15

5. The "Casting Out" Method

Cast out the scorner, and contention shall go out; yea, strife and reproach shall cease.

Proverbs 22:10

The biblical remedy for dealing with scoffers is to cast them out! In modern English, to cast out means to *throw away, to dismiss, to expel, to eject, to banish, to fire, to sack, to discard, to unseat or to lay off.* I believe that almost anyone can understand the meaning of "casting out".

The Bible teaches us to cast out scornful people. A mocker is disloyal to your cause. The biblical treatment for such people is expulsion. Whenever you realize that someone is mocking at you, please do not hesitate to expel him from your life.

Sometimes, failure to dismiss people is like failing to do a surgery that will save your life. I have used this method for treating disloyalty. It was indeed painful, but a new spirit of loyalty entered the church. What a fresh breath of life we all experienced.

When you fail to dismiss someone who must go, you are exhibiting weak leadership. You are allowing a snake to live under your children's bed. Please do not cry if your children are bitten and they die.

6. The Marking and Avoiding Method

Now I beseech you, brethren, mark them which cause divisions and offences contrary to the doctrine which ye have learned; and avoid them. For they that are such serve not our Lord Jesus Christ, but their own belly; and by good words and fair speeches deceive the hearts of the simple.

Romans 16:17, 18

This Scripture teaches that people who cause divisions must be noted and avoided at all costs. What does marking and avoiding mean? **To mark means to brand or to label an object so that it will stand out.** Some sheep need to be branded so that they can be recognized from afar. **It is important to notice a disloyal person from afar.**

I once had to apply this method in dealing with a rebel in my church. Since I could not take a tin of red paint and brand this person, the only way I could mark him was to inform some people that this brother was a doubtful person who should be avoided. I called for a meeting and told them that this brother was unsafe and should be avoided at all costs. By holding that meeting and telling the people that the brother was not loyal to the church, I had branded or marked him sufficiently. I did not even have to give the details of this brother's misdemeanours.

After that, sheep that would have innocently played with that brother became wary of him and stayed off. Indeed, the few sheep that he was able to get close to suffered from his poisonous effusions. There are people who have fallen away today because they were exposed to this person. **Do not be afraid to mark and avoid anyone. It is a biblical instruction given by the Apostle Paul himself.**

When a nation is deporting someone, they often attach a letter that says, "Your presence is now undesirable in this nation." There are some people whose presence is undesirable in the church. They must not be allowed to remain in the church any longer. They must be marked and avoided. They must be expelled and prevented from coming back.

7. The Cursing Method

The Apostle Paul used this method when he was trying to prevent charlatans from deceiving the flock. He was powerless to physically prevent anyone from tricking and dividing his flock. Paul was far away in a Roman prison, so he employed the spiritual method of cursing.

> **But though we, or an angel from heaven, preach any other gospel unto you than that which we have preached unto you, LET HIM BE ACCURSED.**
>
> **Galatians 1:8**

The curse was a spiritual barrier against intruders. When you are powerless in the physical, it is a good method to employ against traitors and mutineers.

Many years ago King David had a disloyal associate called Joab. Joab went against David's commandments and murdered Abner. David realized that it was too risky to fight against Joab. It would have brought more division and destabilized his kingdom. David employed a powerful curse against Joab and his family. He took the matter up spiritually.

David knew that he had power through his tongue, to curse traitors and rebels. And he used it!

> **Let it rest on the head of Joab, and on all his father's house; and let there not fail from the house of Joab one**

that hath an issue, or that is a leper, or that leaneth on a staff, or that falleth on the sword or that lacketh bread.

2 Samuel 3:29

Many years ago, I was preaching in our church. At that time, our church was occupying the medical school canteen in Korle-Bu Teaching Hospital of Accra. I was preaching on the subject The New Wave Churches. At a point nearing the end of my sermon, I began to speak prophetically. **I spoke many prophetic curses against anyone who would rise up to destroy the new wave churches that God was building.**

You see, the Spirit of the Lord upon me was leading me to cover his church with spiritual protection. I believe that those proclamations are at work today! I believe that they contribute greatly to the divine preservation and growth of the ministry!